TO

_____

FROM

_____

DATE

_____

Getting Good at Being You

LEARNING TO LOVE WHO GOD MADE YOU TO BE

LAUREN ALAINA

FOREWORD BY TRISHA YEARWOOD

THOMAS NELSON
Since 1798

Getting Good at Being You

Published in Nashville, Tennessee, by Thomas Nelson. Thomas Nelson is a registered trademark of HarperCollins Christian Publishing, Inc.

Thomas Nelson titles may be purchased in bulk for educational, business, fund-raising, or sales promotional use. For information, please email SpecialMarkets@ThomasNelson.com.

Any Internet addresses, phone numbers, or company or product information printed in this book are offered as a resource and are not intended in any way to be or to imply an endorsement by Thomas Nelson, nor does Thomas Nelson vouch for the existence, content, or services of these sites, phone numbers, companies, or products beyond the life of this book.

Scripture quotations are taken from The Holy Bible, New International Version®, NIV®. Copyright © 1973, 1978, 1984, 2011 by Biblica, Inc.® Used by permission of Zondervan. All rights reserved worldwide. www.Zondervan.com. The "NIV" and "New International Version" are trademarks registered in the United States Patent and Trademark Office by Biblica, Inc.®

ISBN 978-1-4002-2680-1 (HC)
ISBN 978-1-4002-2681-8 (audiobook)
ISBN 978-1-4002-2676-4 (eBook)
ISBN 978-1-4002-3540-7 (Signature edition)

Printed in China

21 22 23 24 25 DSC 10 9 8 7 6 5 4 3 2 1

This book is for any girl out there who could love herself a little more. This is for the girl who has big dreams and a light in her heart that should never be dimmed. I hope whoever and wherever you are, you read this book and realize how imperfectly perfect you are.

CONTENTS

CONTENTS

FOREWORD

I met Lauren Alaina in 2019 at the CMT Awards. A bunch of us "girl singers" had joined together to pay tribute that night to the legendary Tanya Tucker. I was sharing a dressing room with a lot of the newer female artists in country music, but I gravitated to Lauren.

Her laugh and her sense of humor, which were evident right off the bat, drew me in. She was also drop-dead gorgeous but didn't seem to know it, or at least didn't seem to let it get in the way of being real. I liked her immediately.

After the performance, we all went our separate ways, back to our tours, our businesses, our lives. I went back to planning the next season of my cooking show, *Trisha's*

Southern Kitchen. We always have a brainstorming call to talk about potential episode ideas, and I brought up Lauren.

"I don't really know anything about her," I said, "except I think she's one of us." (That's always a big compliment in my book!) Lauren had just released a song called "Getting Good" and I loved it. It reminded me of something I would have recorded earlier in my career, and it spoke to me about loving where you are and not always wishing for what's next. I especially relate to the lyric "Once I learn to grow right where I'm planted, maybe that's when life starts getting good."

So I guess I wasn't surprised that when Lauren came to be a guest on my show, we hit it off and became friends. She brought her manager, Trisha, with her that day. You can tell a lot about a person by who they surround themselves with, and I knew Lauren understood the importance of having the right people in her corner. That day we laughed, cooked, ate, even served fast food as a stunt for the show, and had the best time.

Lauren, at twenty-six-years old, is the same age I was when my first single, "She's in Love With the Boy" came out in 1991. Yeah . . . before she was born, but I'm fine with that! I call her Junior because we have so much in common, from our small-town Georgia roots to our love of a good meal with friends and family. But Lauren has something I never had at her age: wisdom and a strong sense of self. In reading *Getting Good at Being You*, I found myself reliving my own young adulthood, agreeing with so much of what she has to say, and even saying "amen" out loud a lot!

Young people, young women especially, are so hard on themselves and each other. Add celebrity on top of that and it's a train wreck waiting to happen. No wonder so many of us never get to a place where we can fully embrace and accept who we are. Reading Lauren's story reminded me that I'm still that young girl looking for love and acceptance, and I'm almost fifty-seven years old! We never outgrow wanting to fit in, wanting to be enough, but Lauren's book lets us know we're not alone in those feelings and gives us tools to help remind us we are exactly who God wants us to be.

For me, faith is believing in a power greater than myself. God is my true north, and my life is always calmer when I turn the worries and the stresses over to Him (sometimes I forget to do that). It's equally important to say thank You and be grateful when the good things happen. *Getting Good at Being You* encourages you to find your higher power and the strength to get through the bad and to be grateful for the good.

I'm glad Lauren wrote this book for all of us, but I'm even more glad I happened upon this happy-in-her-own-skin gorgeous soul back in that dressing room in downtown Nashville a few years ago. Everybody needs a friend like Junior! When you're reading this book, you'll know she's your friend too.

Love, Trisha

INTRODUCTION

IF I WAS MY BEST FRIEND

*D*o *I love myself?*

I've asked myself that question a lot over the years. Not just, *Do I feel pretty good about me and my choices?* but, *Do I actually head-over-heels, can't-get-enough, shout-it-from-the-hilltops love myself?*

Do you feel that way about yourself? Do you really and truly love yourself?

This is such a difficult question to answer, but I truly feel like I can confidently say that I do—*I love myself.* And getting to this point has been life changing. I have never felt more at home in my own skin and sure of who I am and the life I want to live—but, let me tell you, it has taken *a lot* of work and lessons learned to get here.

I want to share what I've discovered with you because I truly believe that every single one of us is worthy and deserving of wild, beautiful, deeply personal love from ourselves. We should all be cheering ourselves on, taking care of our bodies, speaking to ourselves with kindness, and covering ourselves with grace instead of shame. I want that for you. Don't you?

I truly believe we're all born with inherent love for ourselves. God's love is planted down deep inside our hearts from the start. As little kids, we don't question whether it's okay to be happy, to laugh loud, to get silly, and to live a big life.

Eight-year-old Lauren sure wasn't worried about the stuff she thinks about today! She wasn't shy about putting on her favorite swimsuit and having a good ol' time at the beach, singing karaoke at a party in front of total strangers, or jumping in to play football with the boys. She didn't worry about what others might think, try to dim her light, or push her love for sports to the side so she could be seen as more ladylike. Little Lauren ate when she was hungry and never gave a thought to calorie counting. She took naps when she was tired and flopped down on the couch to chill when she needed some quiet time. If she messed up or hurt someone, she learned to say she was sorry and moved on. She sang her own praises and was her own biggest cheerleader (remember hollering for your parents to watch whatever cool thing you were doing?).

It seems crazy to say, but I knew who I was and what I loved when I was eight a whole lot more than I did fifteen years later. I knew what I loved, what made my heart leap, what made me laugh down deep, and what made me want to sing at the top of my lungs. What were those things for you when you were eight years old?

> **WHAT MADE YOUR HEART *leap* WHEN YOU WERE EIGHT YEARS OLD?**

As I got older, little by little, I began to lose that confidence, that pure joy, that certainty. The world's voice crept in and convinced me that I needed to be thinner, more feminine, quieter, cooler—basically that I needed to be less to be more. How backward is that? Maybe you experienced some of these things too.

If you had asked me when I was twenty how I felt about myself, I would have told you that I loved myself and was grateful for who God made me to be—but I would have been crossing my fingers and toes because of all the exceptions to that statement! It wasn't that I hated certain things about myself. I just believed I could make certain qualities "better" (a.k.a. different) if I tried hard enough. As I grew up, I bought into the lies we're all told as women that we are somehow both too much and not enough all at the same time. And that the only way to be happy and successful is to bend and twist and shrink and grow to fit into a very narrow, confining mold of what a woman "should" be.

As I continued to bend and twist to the world's standards, I couldn't see that in my pursuit to become "perfect," I was seriously letting eight-year-old Lauren down.

WHAT WOULD YOU TELL YOUR BEST FRIEND?

A few years ago, I went through a breakup that nearly broke me. Maybe you've had one of these moments too—where something happens that changes the way you see *everything*. I trusted this guy, saw a real future with him, thought he really understood and appreciated me. Then *bam*! It was over. And we didn't just fizzle out. No, ma'am! We ended in rip-roaring, red-hot flames.

My friends did everything they could to help me move on. They told me that I deserved better, that it was good to realize now that he wasn't the one. All of that was true, of course, but I was too lost in the middle of my emotions to see it. Instead, I kept reliving every aspect of our relationship in my head, trying to pinpoint where I had gone wrong.

One night, my friend Katelyn came over to commiserate over a big ol' stuffed-crust pizza and some wine. She'd been listening to me complain and waffle about getting back together with him for a few hours. She finally turned to me and said, "Lauren, what would you tell me if a guy had treated me the way he has treated you?" Her question stopped me in my tracks.

I looked at her, stunned, pizza forgotten mid-bite. She was right. If a guy had treated *her* this way, I would feel completely different. Instead of second-guessing her every move, blaming her for his betrayal, and berating her for the choices she'd made, I would be reminding her of all the wonderful things about her and telling her how deserving she is of real love. I would be bringing her dinner. I would be hugging her while she cried. And you better believe I'd be taking her out for her favorite brunch or booking a mani-pedi to cheer her up. So why wasn't I doing those things for myself? Why wasn't I being a friend to myself?

Think about the way you love your best friends. Aren't they just the most incredible women? Don't you want *all* the good things for them? And doesn't it break your heart to see them speak badly about themselves? To see them settle for less than the best? You love them exactly as they are! Even the parts they may not love so much! That's how I feel about my friends too.

But I had never considered that I could feel that way about myself.

I realized I had been fumbling in the dark for years. That night, I finally found the light switch. I realized that if I would shift my perspective to see my life from the outside looking in, I could assess it more honestly and objectively. If I would be a friend to myself day in and day out and treat myself the way I treated my friends, I realized I might start to see myself the way I see them. If I would acknowledge that my feelings matter as much as anyone else's, I could embrace those feelings and work through them in healthy ways. If I practiced loving myself and listening to my needs, I could make taking care of myself a habit I'd never want to break. If I worked to love myself, I just might be able to let others love me too.

SHINING A LIGHT

Y'all, why did it take me so long to see that?

It seems so obvious now, but it was truly a revelation that night. It forced me to take a hard look at all the ways I'd been treating myself. I constantly criticized myself, avoided dealing with my feelings, and put my needs squarely in last place in favor of the needs of those around me. Amid this revelation, I realized that if I didn't shine some light on that dark stuff, I'd never be able to really get rid of it.

For example, I used to have a horrible habit of calling myself mean names like *ugly* or *fat* or *stupid*. I was really hateful to myself, which just breaks my heart to think about now. My manager (and one of my very best friends in the world), Trisha, would always say to me, "Don't talk about someone I love like that." I started saying that out loud to myself whenever I caught myself saying something mean. It helped me to notice when I was saying and doing things to myself that I would never say or do to someone else. And if I wouldn't be okay with someone talking to my friends that way, I shouldn't be okay with talking to myself that way either.

I had to really focus on being mindful and noticing

IF WE DON'T

Shine Some Light

ON THE DARK STUFF,

WE'LL NEVER BE

ABLE TO *REALLY*

GET RID OF IT.

when those bad thought patterns tried to sneak back in. When I caught myself pushing my needs aside, trying to squash down my feelings, or holding myself to unrealistic standards, I had to stop and take a few minutes to think about *why* I was being unkind to myself. For me, it almost always came down to not wanting to let someone down or being worried that I wasn't measuring up to someone else's ideas or expectations.

Your *why* will likely be different from mine. Everyone has their own baggage and issues. But I can't stress enough how important it is to do the work to figure it out. Once you know *why* you're struggling to be your own best friend, you'll be able to notice the behavior so much more easily when it pops up to sabotage your day. You'll be able to identify the patterns and habits that feed into that why so you can break them and replace them with new, loving patterns. And most importantly, you'll be able to forgive yourself for all of the times you didn't love yourself the way you deserved.

It's time for all of us to do better. I want you to put this book down and go stand in front of your biggest mirror and have a heart-to-heart with the woman you see there.

Tell her that she is important.

Tell her that she doesn't need to change a single thing to be worthy of love.

Tell her that you love her right now, just as she is.

Tell her that God loves her too.

Tell her that she's beautiful.

Tell her all the reasons she is awesome.

Tell her that God made her unique and that He doesn't make mistakes.

Tell her that you've got her back.

Then make a deal with that girl in the mirror to love on her more, to be kinder, gentler, and more understanding to her. Make being your own best friend your biggest priority. Because that's where it has to start if you want to truly love yourself. You won't be able to switch from bad-mouthing yourself to being deeply in love with yourself overnight, but you can start with simply being the friend you've been needing.

EXACTLY AS YOU ARE

My faith as a Christian has been a huge part of helping me learn to be my own best friend. Knowing and believing that God loves me, exactly as I am, has really helped me

AS YOU BREAK THESE PATTERNS, *you'll be able to forgive* YOURSELF FOR ALL OF THE TIMES YOU DIDN'T LOVE YOURSELF THE WAY YOU DESERVED.

to love myself. I'm going to share a little of that in this book, but if you aren't a Christian, please stick around anyway. This book is absolutely for you too! I have friends who believe similarly, friends who don't, and friends who believe something totally different than I do—and every one of them is equally precious to me. Everyone is welcome here!

We've all heard the Golden Rule, right? Love your neighbor as yourself. It makes sense, doesn't it? Many people don't know that the Golden Rule is actually from the Bible! When people talk about it, they usually focus on the "love your neighbor" part—treat people with kindness, be a good person, and love others the way you'd like others to treat you.

But I think the "as yourself" part is just as important. For whatever reason, when we hear this verse, we see the "as yourself" part as more about how we expect others to treat us—how we want to be treated. Well, shouldn't we have the same expectation of ourselves as we have of others when it comes to how we're treated? And if we were to love ourselves in the ways that we truly, deeply desire, think about how that might open up our hearts to love our neighbors in an even more accepting, authentic, tender, and kind way. If we're talking down to ourselves, not taking care of ourselves, and hating parts of ourselves, well, that isn't love—and we sure wouldn't tolerate that treatment from another person. I don't think Jesus wanted us to treat ourselves or our neighbors like that.

GET TO KNOW YOU

It's just as important to care about ourselves as it is to care about other people. Reread that line as many times as you need to, because it is a truth that so many of us seem to miss. I'm not saying to be selfish—this is really the opposite of that. I'm saying to take the time to get to know *you*, all of you—what makes you tick, what makes you happy, what lights you up inside, what touches your heart. Find the childhood joy and love for yourself that you might have forgotten, and let it back into your heart. As we go through this journey together, I'm going to encourage you to take some steps in each chapter that I've found especially helpful as I've navigated these sometimes messy waters.

When we know and love ourselves fully, we're able to accept love more fully. We're able to understand why someone loves us. When we know and love all the different parts of ourselves, we're able to love others the same way—without judgment, without holding back, unselfishly.

Oh boy, did I need to hear that at eleven, at sixteen, at nineteen, at twenty-four! Each of those Laurens just really needed a hug—big time. If I could go back in time, I'd give each Lauren a big old bear hug—in fact, I'd take a hug right now! Then I'd probably go hug my future self too! I'd tell all of me—past, present, and future—that you get only one life, one chance in this crazy world, and starting out with love is the best way to go.

Embrace the holy hot mess you are—right now. Get to know her. Appreciate her for all that she brings to the table. Love her. Be the kind of best friend to her that she is to everyone else. Treat her with love, kindness, and respect, and then sit back and watch what she can do!

CHAPTER 1

Road Less Traveled

TAKING THE ROAD TO THE REAL YOU

O ne of the greatest gifts you'll ever give yourself is taking the time to get to know yourself, truly and deeply. A girl who knows exactly who she is and what she wants is a force to be reckoned with. A go-getter. A world changer. A fearless champion for herself and others. And a girl who knows herself *and* loves herself? Well, she's pretty much unstoppable.

From the time we're little, we spend most of our lives trying to figure out how to fit in and how to live up to all the expectations around us. Over time, we will stretch to meet goals, try to squeeze ourselves into a smaller role (or even just a smaller pair of jeans!), tone ourselves down, turn ourselves up, and spend way too much time as just "one of the crowd." In that process, it is so, so easy to lose sight of who we really are and to let others dictate for us who we should be and how we should feel.

Oftentimes it feels much simpler to morph into someone you're not than to get to know and like yourself as you are—and possibly rock the boat. It's less complicated just to go with the flow, to fit in, to change yourself in small and big ways to be like everyone else. It seems like it should be the opposite, right? Shouldn't it be easier to be who you are than to try to be someone you aren't? It should! But rebelling, standing up and saying, "This is who I am. I like who I am, and I don't care if you don't," . . . well, that takes serious courage and might ruffle some feathers.

No one wants to let people down, right? So especially when we're still figuring things out, it's much simpler to slip into someone else's expectations for us. Of course, not all of these expectations are bad. Your mom might hope you'll be interested in fashion so you can shop together, or your dad might want you to play basketball because he loves it and would enjoy that time with you. Those don't sound problematic, right? And they're not. The danger is when those expectations clash with who you are and what you desire for yourself.

If you hate basketball but play for years even though your heart is longing to paint, then you've sacrificed something essential to who you are. If the social order at your school is that doing theater is terminally uncool but you've always dreamed of being an actress, you are faced with a tough choice: you can skip the spring musicals in favor of being more popular, or you can grab hold of what you love and star in every play, even if it means you lose social currency.

We are faced with thousands of tiny choices each day that pit who we are against who others want us to be. It may seem like no big deal to make a few small choices that push the real you into the background, but those few small choices add up on top of one another and they lead to more, bigger choices—until one day you wake up and realize that you've become a stranger to yourself.

> WE ARE FACED WITH THOUSANDS OF TINY CHOICES EACH DAY THAT PIT *WHO WE ARE* AGAINST *WHO OTHERS* WANT US TO BE.

WHO IS THAT GIRL?

That's what happened to me. When I made it onto *American Idol* at fifteen years old, I became famous over-night. I traded high school for a full-blown career. I was so grateful and excited, but I was also *completely* unpre-pared. I didn't know how to navigate fame or make deals for myself, so I went along with advice from "experts" who said they knew what was best for me. And because I didn't know myself fully at that point, I let them tell me who to be and lost sight of the real me.

If you had met me as a kid, you never would have expected me to be anything except bold, fearless, and wildly in love with myself. From the time I was six years old and singing karaoke for whoever was in earshot, I'd been telling everyone around me that I was going to be on *American Idol* so they best be ready to vote for me! Little Lauren did *not* lack in confidence. I knew I'd be a singer and songwriter. I had no clue what went into all of that or how much work it would be, but I knew all the way down to my bones that this was my destiny.

So nine years later, when I had the chance to audition for *American Idol* in Nashville, I jumped at the opportunity. I made it onto the show and won second place. It was everything I dreamed it would be, plus so much more. I learned and grew every week when I got up on stage and sang my heart out. Of course, it wasn't easy. Being on *Idol* was hard work, but I couldn't get enough of it. "You were right," I told my inner six-year-old self. "This is what we were made for."

After *Idol*, I went out on tour with the rest of the contestants. I got a manager, signed a record deal, and began my career. It was a whirlwind. I was out of my depth and being pulled in so many directions. I wanted to be a country singer/songwriter, but I didn't know how to make that happen. Which offers should I take? Which songwriters should I work with? What should I say no to? Y'all, the only job I'd ever had was making pizzas at CiCi's, and I dropped like 40 percent of those on the floor! I wasn't really much of a businesswoman at that point, which is why I was thankful that I had a team to help me navigate all of it.

Unfortunately, I didn't have the *right* team. My management team was more concerned with molding me into their idea of what a successful country star should be than who I was as an artist and a person. They told me I needed to change, and let me tell you, they thought I needed to change just about every part of me! Let's just say that this didn't do great things for my self-esteem. I was usually the most outgoing person in the room, so no one would've thought I was insecure, but I definitely was. Is there a fifteen-year-old out there who isn't?

One of my favorite artists of all time is Carrie Underwood. We met during my time on *American Idol*, and she was always kind and encouraging. I really looked up to her. My manager used that to try to get me to change. "If you want to be successful like Carrie, you need to be more like her. You need to lose forty pounds.

You need to make your hair blonder. We've got to change your clothes."

And I listened to her. She was my manager and I thought she knew best! (Spoiler alert: she did not.) I thought, *Oh, my gosh. I have this dream and if I don't work and change to become more like Carrie Underwood, I'll never be successful.*

I went on diets, bleached my hair, and got an entirely new wardrobe. But it still wasn't enough. My manager just found other reasons to criticize me. I didn't even write my first album, which is crazy because I'd been writing songs since I was nine. I let my team talk me into putting out songs from "more experienced songwriters." They were great songs, but they weren't *mine*.

The worse I felt about myself, the more I let others talk down to me and negate my opinions and experiences, which only made me feel even lower. I spent so much time and energy trying to become a "perfect" skinny, blond bombshell singer when I should have been embracing my identity as a curvy, semi-blond songwriter with something big to say with my music (all things I now love about myself by the way).

I was a lost teenager constantly being told that I wasn't enough.

SOMETIMES THE WORSE WE FEEL ABOUT OURSELVES, *THE MORE WE LET OTHERS* TALK DOWN TO US AND NEGATE OUR OPINIONS AND EXPERIENCES.

It wasn't just my management team who had opinions about me and who I should be. Becoming famous overnight meant that I suddenly had fans, young girls who looked up to me and were watching my every move, as well as trolls who jumped on every opportunity to take a shot at me online. People I'd never met were commenting on my weight, my hair, my face, and my wardrobe, and not all of them were nice about it.

My mom has always told me that you can say ten nice things to someone and one mean thing, and all they'll remember is the mean thing. And that was so true for me. I couldn't stop myself from reading all the things people were saying. And it hurt so much to see people making fun of me online. I would also read thousands of other really nice comments, but those never sunk in. The mean ones, though . . . I couldn't shake them.

It took a while, but I finally realized just how far removed I'd become from the me I used to know and love. I needed to be the Lauren *I* wanted to be. Standing up for myself and hiring a new team gave me the confidence boost I needed to start getting back to me. And I knew that I had to figure out what I really wanted from my career and my life before I did anything else.

THE SONG OF YOUR REBEL HEART

Making music and writing songs is really how I got to know myself again. I spent time alone pouring myself into lyrics and melodies, which allowed me to hear my own voice for the first time in a long time. It was just a whisper at first, but it got louder the more I listened. I released six singles during the seven years after *American Idol*. They did fine, but none of them ever took off like I had hoped. I'm grateful for that now. If they'd been hits, I wouldn't have handled it well. I just wasn't prepared. I can see now that I needed to get to know the woman I was growing to be, the parts that had always been with me and the parts that were new and a little wiser for what I had gone through, before I could manage that kind of success well.

The songs I released during those seven years were good songs and they were very *me*, with my point of view and in my style. So of course it hurt when they weren't embraced. But I didn't let that stop me. I wasn't about to give up just because people didn't immediately understand what I was putting out there. I wasn't about to change the music that came from my heart to be more like what was already on the radio. I knew I had to give people time to get to know the real me, not the airbrushed version that my former team had tried to make me into. I truly believed that if I kept releasing my music, people would eventually be drawn to its honesty and connect with the truth I was sharing.

When I wrote and recorded "Road Less Traveled" and it became my first hit, I could say with confidence that I knew myself and that this was the song of my own rebel heart. This was the anthem I wanted to share with other young girls struggling like I had in a world that tries so hard to define us instead of letting us define ourselves. I am still so proud of that song—and even prouder that I believed enough in myself to write it.

> THE PEOPLE OUT THERE *BuilDiNG* LIVES THEY LOVE AREN'T WASTING TIME TRYING TO FIT INTO A MOLD THAT MAKES OTHER PEOPLE MORE COMFORTABLE.

These days, I'm not willing to compromise anything about myself for anyone else. I don't let people put me on diets. I eat what I want. I don't let people pick out my clothes. I wear the clothes I like. I make my own music, and I work with other songwriters who believe in that. I love who I am and the music I'm making, and I wouldn't change a thing.

YOUR ROAD IS WAITING,

AND IT'S ABOUT

TO TAKE YOU

SOMEWHERE BEAUTIFUL.

I understand now that I don't have to be Carrie Underwood. Because Carrie Underwood is Carrie Underwood. And I love her because *she's* Carrie Underwood! And people love me because *I'm* me. The stories and art and work that can really shake things up can't be created if we're too busy trying to be some made-up version of ourselves that other people think we should be. The people out there building lives they love aren't wasting time trying to fit into a mold that makes people more comfortable. They are busting those molds apart with the force of their heart and their personalities and their deep desire to share their passions with the world.

If you feel like you don't know who you are or like you've been trying too hard for too long to be someone you aren't in order to please someone else, it's not too late to change. It's never too late to get good at being you! Keep reminding yourself that you are brave and strong and that God made you special and full of your own unique potential. Owning who you are may make some people angry or disappointed, but that is *way* better than living a life being disappointed in yourself. You don't have to be who anyone else wants you to be. God made you to be you, not someone else.

Every single one of us is on a path to get somewhere in

this life, but you're the only one who can determine your destination. You can follow others to somewhere that was never meant for you, take the road they want you to follow—or you can step out onto the road only you can travel, a road that will take you to the places your heart yearns for. That road is waiting for you, so go ahead and kick up that gravel. It's about to take you somewhere beautiful.

Get To It

Getting to know yourself probably won't happen overnight, especially if you've spent a lot of time trying to be someone you're not. It takes time and space and patience to look within yourself and separate out fact from fiction, to shed the habits and opinions you've picked up from other people, and to replace them with your own authentic motivations and healthier habits that make you genuinely happy.

Not sure where to start? I'm a big believer in writing things down, and I encourage you to write down the answers to some of these questions.

Write out your emotions. I do that through my songwriting. You do what works best for you. Keep a journal, type out your memoir, or write some poetry. You can even write it on your mirror in lipstick if you want to. It doesn't matter if what you write isn't "good." You never have to show your writing to anyone! This is just for you. Here are some questions to get you going:

- When I think of who I am, what are the first five words that come to mind? Why?
- If I had the whole day to myself with nothing I needed to do, how would I spend it?
- When I'm old and gray, which of my dreams would I regret not chasing?
- Who are my favorite people to spend time with? Why? How do they make me feel?
- I'm most comfortable when I'm . . .
- If the house were on fire and I could save only three things, I'd grab . . .

As you write, commit to being really honest with yourself, even if some of your answers seem uncool or embarrassing. Embrace your quirks, your goofiness, the parts of yourself that you think aren't cool—even the parts where you think you might have some work to do. Women who do big things aren't worried about being cool. They are willing to put themselves out there, to be bold, to be foolish, and even to be wrong in order to make history.

Write out all of the parts of yourself that you don't like. Then shake a little love for yourself onto that list. If you wrote, "I hate that I can't seem to shut up," rework it to be "I have a lot to say, and people should be willing to listen." If you wrote, "I'm too emotional," change it to "I have a huge heart and am deeply empathetic, which makes me a good friend."

And then just *keep it up*. Keep reframing these places of pain until you see them as your biggest assets and learn to love yourself and be proud of who you are. It will take time, but it's so worth it. On your way there, if someone's saying something about you that doesn't feel true to who you're learning you are, don't try to force their opinion to fit. I have a friend who likes to say, "What someone thinks of you is none of your business." Ain't that the truth? When we hitch our sense of self-love and self-worth onto what other people think of us, we'll always end up doubting ourselves.

What *is* your business—and what really matters—is what *you* think of you and what *God* thinks of you. And I'm here to tell you that He thinks you're wonderful and amazing. Not everyone on this planet will understand or like everything about you, and that's okay. Just know that if you keep being your most authentic self, you will find your path and the people who will champion you and your journey.

CHAPTER 2

THINK Outside THE Boy

TRUSTING YOUR HEART'S DESIRES

et me paint you a picture . . .

I was eleven years old and in sixth grade. Everyone was obsessed with low-rise jeans and Ugg boots and couldn't stop listening to "Our Song" by Taylor Swift on the radio. I played softball and volleyball and had always been kind of a tomboy, rocking baggy T-shirts and gym shorts so I could play flag football with the boys. You know, just living my best, most awkward preteen life.

But that year something felt different. Those flag football games were interesting for more than just my love of the game. I had my first crush. He was a guy I'd known since kindergarten. We'll call him Logan. Over the summer he'd grown from a skinny kid into a total hottie. He was a football and baseball player, an all-around athlete. He suddenly had muscles and was taller than me. (I towered over a lot of guys in middle school, so that was a big deal.) Combine all of that with dark blue eyes, slightly curly brown hair, and a lopsided grin, and I was totally hooked.

We'd always been really good friends, but that wasn't enough anymore. I wanted him to see me as girlfriend material. Sadly, he did not. In fact, he just about crushed me when he off-handedly mentioned liking a cheerleader. We'll call her Ashley.

I remember thinking, *Why does he like Ashley?* I looked across the playground and spotted her effortlessly doing cartwheels and back handsprings with the rest of the cheerleaders. She was adorable, I had to admit. Ashley had perfectly styled long blond hair, and she wore makeup and the aforementioned fashionable low-rise jeans and Ugg boots. Meanwhile, I don't think I'd even brushed my hair that morning, I was wearing my brother's grass-stained old baseball T-shirt, and my sneakers had a hole in the toe from a particularly rough fall catching the ball. It was quite a look.

Okay, I thought, as everything became clear, *it's time for me to put on some cute jeans and do a cartwheel.* It appeared to me that Logan liked Ashley because she was a cheerleader and was super feminine. If I wanted him to like me, I would have to be more like her. I decided to go over right then and do gymnastics moves next to Ashley. Let's just say I was *not* a natural (I know, shocker!). I was very athletic, but the height and muscles that made me good at softball and volleyball did not translate to toe-touches and effortless cheerleading moves. It was embarrassing, but I was not about to give up. Apparently I have no shame when it comes to getting the guy.

I went home from school that day and told my mom I was quitting softball to be a cheerleader. And I loved softball! But I gave it up for a guy who wasn't even my boyfriend. You might think that all the times I hit my head trying to master that back handspring would've knocked some sense into me, that maybe I didn't like Logan that much after all. Because this *really* was not my thing. But no.

I made the cheerleading squad. But I did not get the guy.

When I was sixteen, I fell for the local bad boy. You

21

know, the one who seems like he stepped right out of a nineties teen movie? We'll call him Spike. Spike basically came with a bad-boy starter pack.

Leather jacket. Check.

Long hair. Check.

Drove a vintage gold Camaro. Played in a rock band. Check. Check.

So I decided I liked all those things too. I swapped out my country boots for Guns N' Roses T-shirts. I think I was in a bit of a rebellious stage. My dad did *not* like this guy, which of course only made me like him more. When Spike said he liked girls with nose rings, I took myself right down to a tattoo parlor and got my nose pierced. I ended up liking the nose ring, but I ended up not liking him so much.

Are you starting to see a pattern here? Hint: changing myself to be what these guys wanted didn't make them love me. I wish I could say I saw it then. But I didn't.

In fact, I was right back at it again until one horrible breakup finally helped me break the pattern. He was the son of a pastor, had grown up in a big, evangelical church, and worked in the Christian entertainment world, and that was intimidating. Now, I am a Christian and I absolutely love the Lord, but I felt completely out of my depth with him. He was so deeply rooted in the Christian world, and he made me feel inferior because I didn't know *all* of the Christian artists, and *all* of the Christian songs, and *all* of the Christian comedians, and *all* of the Christian authors. He put pressure on me to learn about all those things so I could fit in better with his friends. So, of course, it felt like if I didn't learn all of that, he wouldn't love me and respect me.

So I dove deep into my faith. I read all the latest books and devotionals. I went with him to Christian conferences. I learned the Christian entertainment lingo and followed all the big names on social media, drinking in what they had to say to make sure I fit in. Before that, my faith had been more of a private thing between God and me, but now I was shouting it from the rooftops. In a lot of ways, that relationship helped me grow my faith because I did love some of the things I was reading, and a lot of it really inspired me. But I was doing everything for the wrong reasons. I was reading devotionals, praying, and spending time each day in my Bible for the guy instead of doing it because I felt personally drawn into a deeper relationship with God.

When that relationship finally ended, disastrously I might add, I finally realized what I'd been doing for far too long.

CHANGING OURSELVES

ISN'T EXACTLY AN

EFFECTIVE STRATEGY

FOR FINDING REAL LOVE.

DO IT FOR YOU

Long story short, I've spent too much of my not-so-long life losing myself in relationships. My go-to strategy for getting the guy had been to become the girl I thought they wanted me to be. I threw myself into the things they liked—quite literally in the case of cheerleading—and became an expert chameleon. If my crush wanted a girly girl, you'd find me wearing skirts and lip gloss. If he was into running, I'd be jogging my way through six miles a day no matter how my knees felt about it. If he said he hated dogs, I couldn't stand their barking. True story! But I don't hate dogs! I love them! In fact, I adopted my own, an adorable pup named Opry. Take that, Mr. Dog Hater.

It took me far too long to come to the realization that changing everything about myself isn't exactly an effective strategy for finding real love. I mean, if I got the guy, but I lost myself in the process, did I really win?

The problem wasn't that I wanted to like what my crushes liked. We've all done that once or twice, right? My real issue was that I didn't know who I was, and even worse, I didn't believe that *who I was* deserved or was worthy of love. I was trying to define myself by who I was with, but it doesn't work that way. If you change everything about yourself to fit someone else's ideas of who you should be, will you even know how to be with yourself when you're alone? Only you can decide who you really are, and the way to do that is not by trying on interests and personality traits because you think they will earn someone's love.

By pretending to be someone I'm not, I was taking up a space that was never meant for me, and I was allowing some guy to fill a space that was never meant for him. Shouldn't I be holding out for someone who complements my personality? Who fits into my life almost effortlessly, like they've always been there? I want that feeling of coming home to the right person, not living awkwardly in someone's guest room. Don't you?

Don't get me wrong. You can totally be interested in someone else's interests. It's pretty normal to want to learn about what someone new likes when you are getting to know them. But you can't become obsessed with the other person's interests or pretend that you already love those things in order to make them like you. It's great to learn new things. It's great to find different activities to try—you never know, you may just find your new passion by being open to new experiences. But the motivation behind doing that is super, super important. Try new things because you're interested in them or you really want to experience something new. Don't do it because you're trying to conform or change or impress someone to fit into their idea of who you should be.

And it's not just romantic relationships that can bring this out in us. How many times have you seen someone on Instagram or Facebook and felt like if you could just be more like her, your life would be better? If you had her skills and talents or her seemingly easy-to-style hair or were into whatever admirable hobby like her, maybe you'd be cooler, more respected, more interesting, more likable?

Magazines, television shows, social media, blogs, and ads all present us with idealized, airbrushed, overly filtered versions of what it means to be a person in this world, and the messages are all the same: Do this. Try this. Change this. Keep being less of you so you can become more of what we say you should want to be. But why would you want to be what they want anyway?

God didn't place us on this earth to be just like someone else. He didn't carefully select your passions and dreams and purpose for you to throw those away in favor of pretending to be all about whatever someone else likes or says is cool. He didn't fill each of us with unique gifts to watch us waste them just because others don't understand.

God doesn't want us to ignore the callings He has for us in favor of fleeting popularity or passing affection or for likes on social media. Real love, God-sized love will encourage us to grow, to dig deeper into our purpose and to nurture our gifts, to become more fully the people we were always meant to be.

PERMISSION TO LOVE YOU

I took some time in my twenties to stay far, far away from boys and to get to know myself better than I ever had before. I really thought through and invested in what was important to me, what I was passionate about, what made me truly happy, and what made me feel my absolute best. I read my Bible and prayed—because *I* wanted to, thank you very much—and trusted God to show me the paths He was calling me to. And I realized that I'm pretty cool and different and special exactly as I am. I love the woman I have become and am becoming with each new day. And I am absolutely worthy of a love that will see me exactly as I am and *cherish* everything about me, good and bad.

That season of finding Lauren changed everything for

Real Love, God-Sized Love

WILL ENCOURAGE YOU TO GROW,

TO DIG DEEPER INTO YOUR

PURPOSE AND TO NURTURE

YOUR GIFTS—TO BECOME MORE

FULLY WHO YOU WERE ALWAYS

MEANT TO BE.

me. I stopped being so willing to change for someone else. These days, the guy for me loves me for me, quirks and all. And if I have any quirks that he doesn't outright adore, he at least needs to respect them. Just like I want to respect him. I hope we both can enjoy the things that the other enjoys—but that we don't pretend to be anyone but who we already are.

And that goes for friendships too. If I have to pretend to be different just to fit in, then maybe those people aren't for me. Real friends celebrate you and lift you up, honor your interests, and don't make you feel ashamed or weird for being different or standing out. In fact, real friends want you to stand out for being your amazingly awesome self, so get good at being you!

Once you love yourself, you'll give everyone around you permission to do the same. I promise you that there are people out there who will love and accept you *exactly as you are*. And you will love and accept them for who they are. Those are your people—your best friends and your love of a lifetime! You can explore their interests with them, but you won't have to change a thing about yourself for them to see how wonderful you are. You aren't exactly like anyone else, which means that you have something to contribute to this world that no one else can.

If you don't love yourself enough to be you and make that contribution, the world loses. We all miss out on hearing your story and seeing what you were made to do.

If you're a softball player, be a softball player and show 'em what you've got. If you're a cheerleader, hit those jumps! If you don't want a nose ring, your nose will look great without one. If you do want a nose ring, what are you waiting for? Go do it! We owe it to those who do and will love us to love ourselves fully and to be unapologetically who we truly are.

Get To It

Are you exhausted from bending yourself into pretzels trying to be something other than yourself—someone besides the real, true you? I see you, girl! It's time to let go of the fear that you aren't worthy just as you are. It's time to think outside what the boy or the world or social media says. Take the time to find yourself and to take hold of who you are—because you're so special! Get to know you, everything about you. Figure out what you love about you and *own it*. I know that can be easier said than done, but here are a few ideas to get you started. I am a big fan of making lists; you should give it a try!

- *Get out a notebook and start making some lists!* Writing down things you know about yourself deep down will help give you some insight into other areas you might not have given much thought.
  - List your strengths.
  - List your favorites—movies, food, music, books, TV shows, hobbies, and anything else you can think of!
  - List places you want to travel to and why.
  - List things you want to accomplish in your life.
  - List your favorite people to spend time with.
  - List what you would do if you won a million dollars.

- List the wonderful traits about your closest friends.
- List what makes *you* a good friend.
- List what you really want in a romantic partner.

• *Date yourself for a while.* Take yourself out to dinner, to movies, to concerts. Go rock climbing or take cooking classes or check out an escape room or spend a day at a park or museum. Keep trying new things to figure out how you really like to spend your time.

• *Reassess how you spend your time now.* Check in to make sure you're actually spending your time in ways *you* want to and in ways that fill you up.

- Do you really love running marathons or are you over it?
- Do you put award-winning movies in your Netflix queue but keep choosing to rewatch old episodes of *The Office* instead?

- Does your weekly book club bore the heck out of you?
- Are you tired of pretending to love something that everyone else seems to like?

- *Let yourself evolve.* Just because you're super into baking bread this year doesn't mean you have to love it forever. So what if you've played violin for the last fifteen years? If it doesn't fill you with joy anymore, take a break or quit altogether. It's okay if your interests grow and change as you do.

- *Don't forget to dream.*
  - What dreams do you know deep down that you have to go after?
  - What is holding you back?
  - If you failed, could you try again? Would you?
  - What would be the worst thing that happened if you failed?
  - What if you succeeded? How would that change things for you?

— Keep a journal. Document your feelings, your experiences, and your plans as you chase your dreams. When you find yourself getting swept up in someone else's expectations, you can go back and reread for a solid dose of the real you.

Be proud of all your amazing qualities and strengths. Go all in on the things you love and are passionate about. Take the time to create a life you love for yourself, where you are truly comfortable. It might take some time and work to figure it all out, but it will be worth it.

CHAPTER 3

PRETTY

REDEFINING BEAUTY

I don't know a single woman who doesn't light up when someone tells her she looks pretty. But what even is pretty anyway? Can you measure it? Is it the same for everyone? I can tell you that my definition probably isn't the same as yours, and yours probably isn't the same as other people's. I can't help wondering why we all try *so* hard to be pretty when we can't even seem to agree on what it means. Do we all truly believe that something outward like "pretty" can be *achieved* if we just try

37

hard enough? And what do we expect it to accomplish if we do achieve it?

Well, I can tell you a few things I know for sure: the true definition of pretty isn't the size of your jeans, the dress you have on, the fullness of your lips, or the color of your eyes or your skin or your hair. *Pretty* is how you treat people. Pretty comes from your heart.

One of the things I've struggled most with in my life is feeling pretty. Redefining that word and deciding that my outward appearance is not what determines the amount of beauty I possess has been one of the biggest challenges I face. I have had to tell myself again and again that *pretty* is how I carry myself, how I treat people, how I love myself, and how I love others.

My struggle with pretty has always been about my weight and my body. The struggle is different for everyone. I'm sure you have something about your appearance that you don't like from time to time—or maybe, like me, you don't like it *most* of the time. Trust me, I get it and I have no judgment. I get what it feels like to not feel good about yourself. I understand what it feels like to convince yourself that if you can just control or change your appearance enough, you'll be worthy of love and admiration.

PRETTY IS HOW
YOU TREAT PEOPLE.
*PRETTY COMES FROM
YOUR HEART.*

PRETTY DIFFERENT

The first time I remember noticing that my body was shaped differently from other girls' was in fifth grade. I hosted a slumber party and had a bunch of girls from my class over. My mom had one of those adhesive strapless bras air-drying in our laundry area. I guess the girls at my party had never seen one of those before, and they thought it was something else. When I went back to school Monday, a rumor was swirling around that I wore butt pads. I didn't even know what butt pads were! We were only nine or ten years old. Why would any fifth-grader be wearing butt pads? I went home that afternoon in tears and asked my mom, "Do I look different from other people?"

My mom was so great. She told me that I was beautiful just the way God made me and that God created us all differently. She assured me that I really didn't want to be just like everyone else, but at that moment in time, that's exactly what I wanted. I wanted to fit in, to have the slim hips and small waists that the other girls did. I didn't want to be different. That was where my struggle began—wanting to fit in and look like the skinniest girls at my school or the models on the covers of magazines.

Right then, in fifth grade, I got the message loud and clear that pretty equals skinny, and I would believe that lie for the next decade of my life.

As I moved up to middle school, I was well on my way to being obsessed with being thin. It's so heartbreaking to me now to look back at little Lauren and think, *I just wish you could know that when you're twenty-six, you're going to celebrate your body—curves and all—and be so proud of the body you have.* But I definitely didn't feel that way at ten years old.

I already told you I became a cheerleader the following year. It was both very fun and very difficult for me. I had an athletic build and was tall for my age, but most of the other girls had been doing gymnastics for years and were petite and slim. As the tallest on the team, I was always put in the back, which only fueled my insecurities. I wanted to be shorter. I wanted to be thinner. I wanted my legs and booty to look like the other girls' did in our cheerleading skirts. I was really insecure.

A few months into the school year, in health class, we watched a video about the dangers of eating disorders. The girl in the video struggled with anorexia and bulimia, and it showed her purging her food. That was a lightbulb moment for me—but not for the reason they intended. I remember thinking, *So that's how you do it. She purges her food and she's thin, so that's how I'm gonna do it too.*

How sad is that? The girl in this video was so sick that she was hospitalized, but all I saw was that she was thin. I immediately started eating healthier foods like she had, but at twelve years old, it's difficult to avoid junk food and pizza forever. So whenever I ate something unhealthy, I'd purge afterward. I wouldn't say I was fully active with my bulimia until I was a bit older, but age eleven was the first time I tried it out.

PRETTY PRESSURED

A few years later, I gained weight after having to take several rounds of steroids for an unrelated health issue. That was the summer I auditioned for *American Idol*. I was fifteen years old, the youngest contestant by far, and going through my most awkward stage on national television. We all go through that tricky time during puberty when our bodies are changing quickly and we have both baby fat and boobs. Well, that was me. I was still just a kid and it showed. In fact, I wore my hair scrunched up with hairspray and a rainbow dress with a matching rainbow necklace with rhinestone flip-flops for that audition. Can we just take a minute to appreciate our fifteen-year-old selves and how bold we were with our fashion choices?

I hated how I looked on that audition tape and immediately began trying to lose weight, dropping twenty-two pounds by the end of filming. But that didn't stop the flood of hateful comments about my weight from people online. One blog referred to me only as "Miss Piggy" and photoshopped a pig snout and ears onto every picture of me. Imagine seeing that as a fifteen-year-old girl. With all of that combined, my eating disorder took a serious turn for the worse.

It only became worse after *American Idol*. I was constantly criticized about my weight, and my management team put me on an extremely restrictive diet. I had to give myself shots every morning to increase my metabolism and was allowed to eat a *very* limited number of calories each day. Of course, no one knew that I was also purging those precious few calories. It didn't go entirely unnoticed, though. My mom was on tour with me, and she began to realize that I was struggling. She confronted me about how I was doing, but I lied and swore there was

CAN WE JUST TAKE
A MINUTE TO
APPRECIATE OUR
FIFTEEN-YEAR-OLD
SELVES AND
HOW BOLD WE WERE
WITH OUR
FASHION CHOICES?

no issue. I'm sure she felt completely helpless watching me become more and more unhealthy. I had lost over forty pounds, was down to a size 0, and was losing my hair in clumps. I was so, so sick.

Around that time, I began to notice my voice becoming strained. I was struggling to hit notes that had always been easy, and my throat was often sore. My mom finally made me a medical appointment with a specialist. After some tests, he told me that I had polyps on my vocal cords and that my vocal cords were actively bleeding. His next question was, "Have you ever had an eating disorder?"

I was really confused why he would ask me that. He was a throat specialist, not a nutritionist. My eating habits were none of his business. I lied and said no. But my mom was in the room and she did that very mom thing you've probably experienced. She gave me *a look*. And in her I-already-know-the-truth-so-you-might-as-well-just-admit-it mom voice, she said, "Lauren."

Until that moment, I really thought I'd been hiding it from her. I burst into tears and admitted everything—the skipping meals, the hiding food so I didn't have to eat it, and the purging, so much purging. I felt so ashamed and embarrassed.

That was rock bottom for me. The doctor told me that if I didn't stop purging immediately, I could very quickly destroy my vocal cords forever. The realization that I might never be able to sing again got through to me in a way that nothing else could have. It terrified me. Singing meant everything to me. I knew I had to change my habits and start taking care of myself.

My mom stepped in and took charge. She whisked me away to a beach house for a few weeks so we could get to the bottom of everything I'd been hiding. Every morning, she'd stand me in front of the mirror and make me say three things I loved about myself. When we started, I couldn't say a single thing. Not one thing. I remember staring in the mirror and crying because it revealed just how out of control my problem was. That realization finally started me down the right path. That year became a reset year for me and was the beginning of my recovery.

THE *HARDesT* PART ABOUT HAVING AN EATING DISORDER IS THAT IT WORKS.

The hardest part about having an eating disorder is that it works. I wanted to be thin, and I was. I was the thinnest I'd ever been. People complimented me. Articles were written praising my weight loss. Everyone seemed so impressed that I was skinny. I was disappearing, but even at my thinnest, I never felt pretty.

PRETTY HONEST

The truth is that the size of my body was never the problem. The problem was *how I felt about myself.* The calorie restriction and bulimia were symptoms of the fact that I didn't love—or even like—who I was, who God made me to be. I was more surprised than anyone to realize that recovering from my eating disorder was much less about food than it was about learning to see the good in myself, to know who I truly was, and learning to love myself, flaws and all.

I am no longer active in an eating disorder, but it will always be something I struggle with. And that's okay. It's a part of who I am. Everyone has their struggles, and this is one of mine. Maybe your struggles are similar to mine. Maybe they're totally different. But they're part of your story, and that matters. They're part of who you are . . . and they're part of how you grow.

If you find yourself, like I did, hating just about

everything about yourself, I want you to know that you aren't alone. What do you see when you look in the mirror? Or when you look at your heart? It might be a difficult exercise (it sure was for me). But I promise good things are there, even if you can't see or feel them. It's like you've been looking into a funhouse mirror at the fair, the one that makes everything all blurry and distorted and out of proportion so it's impossible to see yourself clearly. Just know that that's not real! And whatever feelings you're having that are painful or overwhelming, please don't keep them to yourself.

Get with the person you trust most and share your heart. Ask them to tell you what they love about you. I know this might seem weird, but I'm telling you, the people who love you *really love you* and want to tell you these things! Things like, "You have amazing eyes" or "You tell the best jokes" or "Your laugh makes the whole room light up."

Write down what they say and stick these notes on your bathroom mirror so you can see them every day. Say them out loud to yourself. It helps to hear out loud all the ways others think you're pretty—and the kind of pretty that really matters. Saying these reminders to yourself will help you begin the process of speaking to yourself in gentler and kinder ways. I can't promise that you'll feel different overnight, but I know you'll start to see yourself more clearly if you keep it up.

PRETTY SUPPORTED

If you're struggling, get a counselor or therapist! I've gone to therapy for years, and I probably always will. No one hands us an instruction manual on being a human. It's okay to need some help! I'm convinced that good therapists are gifts from God. There is no shame in needing to talk to someone objective, someone who is trained to help give perspective. In fact, getting help is one of the bravest, kindest things you can do for yourself.

My therapist has helped me change how I think about my body, how I talk to myself, and which words I use to describe myself. I know counseling can be expensive, but there are many options out there. Look into online resources. If you're in school, ask a trusted teacher or the school counselor for help. (If you're in college, resources may be available through student services.) If you attend a church, most likely someone who works there provides just this kind of help to attendees. And a number of counselors offer a sliding scale based on what you can afford. Just remember that there are options out there, and it's worth the effort to find someone who can help.

YOU ARE ENOUGH

A few months ago, as I was getting ready for an award show, for the first time in a very long time, I used the word *fat* to describe myself. I didn't feel good in the dress I'd chosen for that night. The word came out of my mouth, and I immediately regretted it. *I don't talk to myself like this. I need to check in with myself and see why I feel this way.*

I was feeling afraid of being judged on the red carpet. My dress wasn't the problem; my fear was. So I took some time to work through those feelings. I let that fear go, put on the dress, and felt beautiful that night. I never could have done that six years ago. I've come a long way.

We all have our insecurities, and I think many of them are born out of fear. We see how harshly the world judges women. We see those impossible standards for what the world says is beautiful. And we fear that we will never measure up, never be *enough* to be considered pretty.

MY HEART IS AS
BIG AND PRETTY
AS THEY COME.
I KNOW YOURS IS TOO.

Whether your *enough* is small enough, tall enough, short enough, or curvy enough, I promise you that getting to that enough won't change anything until you change the definition of *pretty* for yourself. My definition of pretty when I was sixteen and my definition at twenty-six are completely different, and I'm really proud of that.

I still have days when I don't feel great about myself. Let's be honest, we all have those days. But on those days, I try to think about ten-year-old Lauren the Monday after that slumber party, the one who felt like her body stood out when she just wanted to fit in. I'm still that same Lauren, with a body that stands out for being different than the other girls' in country music and in my industry in general. The difference now is that I feel pretty from the inside out. I'm not the thinnest I've ever been by any means. And that's okay—because my weight doesn't determine my worth. I love myself, and the people around me love me. And the last time I checked, the people who love me don't love me for the size of my jeans. They love me for the size of my heart and how I treat them.

And my heart is as big and pretty as they come. I know yours is too.

Get To It

What if I asked you to redefine *pretty* for yourself? What if the good work you do in your community has you at supermodel status? What if the tenderness you show yourself and others lands you on magazine covers? Or what if the uplifting ways you counsel others makes you the next Miss America?

We can redefine *pretty* to mean all of those things, you know, but each of us has to start by seeing ourselves that way. Small changes can make a big difference when it comes to treating ourselves in pretty ways. (Don't forget to grab your journal!)

- Start by doing what my mama made me do. Go stand in front of your mirror, and say three things you love about yourself. Go on . . . I'll wait. Okay, good!
  - How did that feel? Easy or difficult? Why?
  - Did you say things about your body? Your heart? Both?

- Could you have said more than three things?

I want you to do this exercise every single morning. You may feel silly at first, but I think it's really important to encourage ourselves. Start each day by telling yourself how pretty you are on the inside, and eventually you'll start to see it on the outside.

- Take care of the body you're in, even if you don't feel pretty that day.
  - Get a good night's sleep each night.
  - Drink plenty of water.
  - Exercise in healthy ways.
  - Feed your body food that will fuel it.
  - Speak kindly to your body and celebrate how unique it is.
  - Do things each day that make you truly, genuinely happy, things that make you feel good.
- Talk to your friends or your mom or a therapist about your least pretty feelings. Be

honest about your struggles. Getting all of that out into the light will help keep the darkness from building up inside you. You don't have to deal with your pain and insecurities alone.

- Ask your friends what makes you truly pretty, and write their answers down.
- Have your family members tell you their favorite things about you, and write those answers down too.
- Talk to your boss about your strengths and where you excel. Write all of it down.
- Have your significant other write down how they feel about you.
- Read these things out loud to yourself often to help you see what the people who love you see.
- Find an affirmation statement that works for you. It doesn't have to be complicated, just a short phrase or sentence you can say to yourself when

you're struggling with feeling your best. If you say it enough, I promise you'll start to believe it. Here are a few examples to get you started.

- I am pretty, inside and out.
- My heart makes me gorgeous.
- God made me beautiful.
- Pretty is as pretty does.
- Pretty cares and pretty loves.
- I am a light burning bright.
- People are drawn to my beautiful heart.
- I am confident and radiant.

Once you say your statement, do your best to live like you believe it. It will help more than you know!

I know how intimidating it can be to go from hating just about everything about yourself to trying to love yourself. If someone like me, who used to have such a poor opinion of myself, can change that perspective, you can too. And trust me, it is so worth it in the end.

CHAPTER 4

Doing Fine

BREAKING THROUGH THINKING YOU'RE BROKEN

huge part of learning to love myself was learning to be honest about my story, even when it wasn't comfortable. I grew up believing that there are just some things you don't talk about, that certain struggles should always be kept secret or private—because they're either shameful or embarrassing. I assumed that if everyone knew all of my most messiest secrets, they wouldn't love me anymore. I bet you've felt that way about certain things too.

My family kept plenty of secrets over the years too. Little ones, like the fact that we love mashed potato sandwiches (hey, don't knock it till you try it!) and some big ones too. The biggest was probably my father's struggle with alcohol. I don't remember anyone ever telling me not to talk about it. It was just understood that this was family business, not for outsiders. Growing up the daughter of an addict meant I learned younger than many that life is uncertain. Dad had good days, but he also had very, very bad days, and I never knew which kind of day it was going to be.

When you live with someone whose behavior is unpredictable like that, you learn to work around it, to adapt to the situation at hand. But you usually don't realize that other people don't jump through the same hoops you do. Once I knew that other people's dads didn't drink excessively, I wasn't about to tell them that my dad did. My home life wasn't normal, so that might mean my family wasn't normal. What if they thought I wasn't normal—that there was something wrong with me? And didn't want to be my friend anymore? So I kept quiet.

My dad was in the army before he married my mom, and he had pretty severe PTSD (post-traumatic stress disorder) from those years in the service. A few drinks after work took the edge off. Then, when I was six, his dad, my grandfather, took his own life. To say that my father was devastated would be an understatement. Losing a parent is difficult even when you're mentally prepared. But you can't prepare for this kind of thing. My dad tried to drown his pain in beer and liquor. It didn't take the pain away, but it did let him forget for a little while. The problem was that as time went on, it took more and more alcohol to blunt all of that pain and anxiety—until Dad reached a point where he couldn't stop, even when he wanted to.

He tried to hide it for a long time, insisting that his drinking was not a problem. He thought he was okay because he was a hard worker who got up and went to his job every day. After all, he wasn't falling down drunk in public or drinking at work. But that thing that was "not a problem" infiltrated every aspect of our lives. It was "not a problem" that Dad swung by the gas station for beer every night and then came home and drank them all until he stumbled to bed or passed out on the couch. It was "not a problem" that we never knew if Dad would be fun-loving after a few drinks or if he would be mean and hard. It was "not a problem" when he'd pick fights with my mom because he was drunk.

DOING FINE

All of those "not a problems" for him were big problems for the rest of us.

When I went to friends' homes and saw their dads go all night without a drink or opened their fridge and didn't see a single beer inside, well, it made me wonder why my daddy drank and so many others didn't. My mom said we needed to pray for Daddy, so I did—all the time. I also poured out all of my dad's beers and wrote "Jesus loves you" on the labels one time. I probably don't have to tell you that that stunt didn't go over too well! As I got a little older, I understood that I was not in control when it came to my dad's drinking. Everything about our family's life could have been perfect, straight out of my dad's wildest dreams, and my dad still would have been an alcoholic. My father was *addicted* to alcohol. It wasn't something he could just stop doing—not without help.

KEEPING THE PEACE

I often felt like I had to hide whatever I was going through. Friends who hadn't been to my house *never* would have known that my dad drank. My friends who did know my dad drank didn't know just how bad it really was.

61

And I found myself drowning in all these secrets. At times I felt desperate to confide in someone, *anyone*, how scary it was when my mom and dad would start yelling at each other or how my dad's eyes would change with each subsequent drink—until he felt like a stranger sitting in my daddy's favorite chair. But I felt like no one would understand, so instead, I kept my feelings to myself and prayed every night that God would help my dad stop drinking.

HAVE YOU EVER FELT YOURSELF *DROWNING* IN SECRETS?

Once I made my debut on *American Idol*, the whole family doubled down on our secrecy, all without even discussing it. I had a shiny, new all-American girl image to preserve, and a dad who drank a bottle a night did not fit with that image. Behind the scenes, I did everything I could think of to help my dad get sober, but "everything a teenager can think of" isn't exactly the help an alcoholic really needs. The more I pestered my dad to quit, the more strained our relationship became. We went long stretches of time without speaking much at all. And when we did talk, our conversations didn't progress much beyond:

"Hi, Dad. How are you?"

"Doing good, baby girl. How are you?"

"Oh, fine. Just busy with performing and everything."

"Well, that's good, sweetie. I love you and sure am proud of you."

"Love you too, Dad. Bye."

I knew that my dad loved me and was proud of me. I *never* doubted that. I loved him too. And I knew he was in pain. I just didn't know how to help him.

WHEN THINGS DON'T MAKE SENSE

After *Idol* ended, I went on tour with the rest of the contestants. I was only sixteen, so my mom traveled with me for the better part of two years, leaving my dad and my brother, Tyler, back home in Georgia. She sacrificed a lot to do that with me, and in a lot of ways, it meant that she and my dad lived very separate lives. When I was eighteen and on my way to recovery for my eating disorder, my mom went home and told my dad she wanted a divorce. She was ready to move on. She went on later to marry my stepdad, Sam, one of the best men I've ever known.

At the end of the day, the divorce was the right thing for my parents.

But I couldn't see that right away. I was crushed. I'd just never considered the possibility that my parents wouldn't make it. I guess I should have seen it coming. Most happily married couples don't fight like my parents did. But I wasn't mentally prepared for that blow. Even though I was eighteen, little Lauren still felt a lot of this pain. I couldn't picture us opening presents around the Christmas tree without my dad in his favorite chair, drinking a cup of black coffee. Or watching the Macy's Thanksgiving Day parade with Dad without my mom fussing around in the kitchen, putting the turkey in the oven. I couldn't imagine not having all of us in one place for life's biggest moments.

How I felt, though, was nothing compared to how my dad felt. The divorce sent him spiraling until he finally hit rock bottom. Losing his marriage forced him to see how destructive his drinking had been. When he couldn't stop on his own, he ended up in rehab. My entire family drove him down together. It was the quietest, tensest car ride we've ever had as a family. After a grueling month facing down his demons and his addiction, Dad walked out a freer man than he'd been since he was a teenager. He's been sober ever since.

WHEN THE TRUTH HURTS

I was happy for my dad and so, so proud of him. But I also felt really embarrassed and ashamed to admit what my family was going through. I was very much in the public eye, trying to save face, when *I* wasn't even sure how I felt about it all. I didn't want interviewers to ask me about my family or to tell friends that my parents had divorced, or that my dad had been in rehab, or that my mom had moved on quickly and married an old family friend.

I didn't want to talk about it or think about it—which meant, of course, it was all I could think about.

I had a writing session booked with Emily Shackelton and busbee, two veteran Nashville songwriters. Songwriting, by its very nature, requires you to be honest and vulnerable about your feelings. On that day, I ended up pouring out my heart when they asked how I was doing. I shared all of my conflicting feelings and how embarrassed I was at how messy my family was right then.

When I was all talked out, Emily turned to me and said, "Hey, you don't have to be ashamed of your story. We're all a little broken. We're all doing the best we can. We're all trying to get where we're going."

That phrase, "we're all a little broken," really cut to the heart of it for me. It just so happened to be a ready-made song lyric, but it also helped me realize that I had mistakenly been clinging to a false belief that I had to hide my struggles to be worthy of love and that no one else would ever understand what I was going through. Since more than 10 percent of adults in America suffer with Alcohol Use Disorder and nearly half of marriages end in divorce, logically, *a lot* of people out there knew exactly how I felt! I suddenly realized that a lot of my fans could probably relate to my struggles. I wanted to stop pretending and get honest about what I was going through. Emily, busbee, and I took that conversation and wrote "Doin' Fine."

IT'S OKAY NOT TO BE OKAY

Taking that first step and putting something messy and personal into my music was scary. I'm still not sure exactly what terrifying thing I thought was going to happen, but nothing bad happened at all.

Instead, something amazing occurred.

My fans started telling me their messy stories.

Their stories of overcoming trauma and pain and big challenges I couldn't even dream up were so inspiring. And you know what? To me, their stories made them *more worthy* of my love and respect, not less. This is the stuff we should all be sharing with each other.

The truth is that each and every person you meet is going through some stuff you don't know about. People don't just walk up to you and tell you all the traumatic things that have happened to them. No one just *volunteers* their biggest mess-ups and most shameful weaknesses, but we all have those things, every single one of us. When I am able to be brave and put my struggles and my issues and my most honest self out there, I make it okay for someone else to do the same thing. I don't want to live my life feeling like I need to cover up parts of who I am or the life I've lived so far. And I don't want the people in my life to feel that way either. I want my relationships to be based in authenticity and honesty, even if it's ugly or difficult or uncomfortable sometimes. I'd take that any day over a pretty lie.

We're all trying to appear to the outside world as the best version of ourselves, which is great, but I think sometimes we lose sight of the fact that it's okay to be going through things or that parts of our stories aren't

OUR STORIES MAKE US

MORE WORTHY

OF LOVE AND

RESPECT, NOT LESS.

necessarily ideal—things that make us feel foolish or ashamed or that we just plain wish we could write out of our lives, thank you very much.

The details of our stories are all different, but the core has way more in common than you might think. We all experience heartache and grief, happiness and sadness, joy and pain, success and failure. I know the gut instinct to paint a pretty picture and make it look like everything is perfect, but nothing and no one is perfect. And even if your life *were* perfect, it wouldn't be nearly as beautiful and interesting as the messy, wild, unpredictable story you're living right now.

ON THE OTHER SIDE

My family's story has turned out to be a beautiful one of forgiveness and second chances. My parents have been able to forgive each other, and my brother, Tyler, and I have been able to forgive them too. Addiction, secrecy, fighting, and divorce can cause a lot of hurt and emotional scars over time. I'm grateful that we've all had the chance to heal. My mom and dad still care about each other. Since their divorce, they have both had the chance to experience a new life with new chapters. They are both happier and healthier, and I am so proud to be their daughter.

Maybe you're reading this and still stuck in the middle of your hot mess of a story. Maybe you've been praying for forgiveness or trying to find the courage to be honest with the people you love, but for whatever reason, the healing you're hoping for just hasn't happened yet. I want to encourage you to hang on. Life and relationships are messy, but when you are brave enough to put your most authentic self out there, you can almost always find a way to clean up that mess. Remember when I recommended counseling earlier? That's still a good idea. But it will also help to talk to a friend, write in your journal, or even scribble down your feelings into a song or a poem. Just tell your story the best way you can. In the process, you may find the healing you've been seeking.

Wouldn't it be a relief to stop pretending everything is okay all the time? To let your guard down and just be yourself? It gets exhausting trying to pretend that everything is perfect. I'm not perfect, but the people who know me love me anyway. And my family isn't perfect either, but they're my family and I love them exactly as they are. You aren't perfect, but you are still absolutely worthy of the biggest and best love out there.

Our stories are our stories. What happens to us does define us, but it doesn't have to define us negatively—or forever. You get to decide what your story says, how the next chapter is written, the ending you want to strive for. You're still in the middle of it all—we all are! A hard season doesn't mean that something really beautiful can't come on the other side. Adversity helps us grow and makes us stronger. Grief makes us more empathetic and caring. Loss helps us become more grateful. Every hardship I've ever gone through I've been able to get to the other side of it and write a new chapter.

Our stories are what we make them. So let's write a good one.

Get To It

"Doin' fine" doesn't have to be the stock answer we give when someone asks how we're doing. We don't have to gloss over our problems. Ultimately, I want you to get to a point where you can say you're doin' fine and really mean it. A huge part of that is letting go of the need to appear perfect and to embrace where you are in your journey.

I finally started to actually feel fine about my story when I got honest about what I was going through. *Fine* wasn't a traditional family in a house with a white picket fence. For me, *fine* was parents who divorced and remarried and a dad who completed rehab. *Fine* wasn't fixing everyone in my family; it was loving them, flaws and all, and choosing them even when it was difficult.

Let's figure out what *fine* means for you. Start with whatever you're struggling with right now. You already know what it is—it's that issue that's been living large (and rent-free!) in your brain for too long. It's time to get it out of the shadows and into the light.

- *Tell the story.* Write it out, type it into the notes app on your phone, or voice record it. It doesn't matter how you get it out; it just matters that you get the story out of your heart and into a form that you can look at a little more objectively.

- *Take a long, hard look.* Which parts of what you wrote are you the most embarrassed about or ashamed of?
- *What can you do?* You obviously can't change what's already happened, so what can you do now to heal, to move forward? Pray about it. I promise that there is something you can do that will help soothe your soul.
  - Is there anyone you're ready to forgive?
  - Do you need to apologize to someone?
  - Can you volunteer or raise money for an organization related to what you've gone through?
  - Can you make changes in your life to prevent something like that from happening again?
  - Is there something you started but never finished? It's time to finish it now.
  - Do you see patterns that

contributed to what happened?
How can you disrupt those patterns
to make new, healthier ones?

− Can you share your story with
others to give them hope or help
them see they aren't alone?

- *Now do it.* Once you have a plan, it's
time to actually carry it out. If it helps,
enlist a friend to come alongside you.
We don't have to do these things alone!
Taking charge and moving forward to
find a way to close out this chapter on a
healing note will make a big difference
toward helping you find *fine* for yourself.

CHAPTER 5

The Bad Guy

THERE'S NOTHING WRONG WITH HIM NOT BEING MR. RIGHT

It's fairly easy to make the right decision when you're faced with an obviously bad situation and an obviously good one, right? But life doesn't always give us such black-and-white choices. Many times, we have to choose between a good situation and *another* good situation. Or maybe we have to choose to leave a good situation behind because it's good but it's not the *right* situation. And that's a lot more challenging.

I know I keep saying this, but that's why it's *so impor-tant* to truly know and love yourself. You are the only one who can decide what's right for you, and you will have to make these kinds of decisions over and over and over again in life. If you don't know yourself and aren't your own biggest champion, it's so easy to settle for a pretty good situation instead of fighting for the amazing situa-tion you really want and deserve. Whether it's a job you're good at but don't love, a school that's fine but also not your first choice, or a safe, pleasant existence that isn't the life you've always dreamed of, it takes strong belief in yourself to walk away from a sure thing, a safe thing, to take a chance for something better.

It might break your heart to let someone down or to leave something comfortable and safe, but you owe it to yourself to stay true to your dreams. It's up to you to know which things are worth fighting for and which are worth letting go of. You have to know your own mind and heart and be willing to disappoint others to protect that precious part of you.

Sometimes you have to be the bad guy to be the good guy for yourself.

IT TAKES STRONG BELIEF

IN YOURSELF TO WALK

AWAY FROM A SAFE THING

TO TAKE A CHANCE FOR

SOMETHING BETTER.

WHEN YOU NEED TO BE THE BAD GUY

I've had a few of those bad-guy moments over the years, but the biggest by far was when I broke off my engagement with my former fiancé, Alex. Ending that relationship was one of the most difficult choices I've ever made. It was absolutely the right decision for so many reasons, but it felt so heavy and hard and painful when the choice was in front of me. It broke my heart to say goodbye because I truly loved him, but I knew I wasn't the right girl for him. One of us was going to have to step up and be the bad guy.

Alex and I started dating when we were seventeen and were together for a little over six years. He supported me through launching my career after *American Idol* and overcoming my eating disorder. We went to his prom together and danced all night. I was there when he graduated from high school, and we celebrated together when he got into college. We made the move to Nashville together. He helped me get settled into my apartment, and I helped him get settled into his dorm room. He held my hand and let me cry on his shoulder when my parents announced their divorce and when my dad made the decision to go to rehab. I helped him study and cheered the loudest when he graduated from college. We celebrated holidays and birthdays and all the little excitements in life side by side. He was a part of my family, and I sure felt like a part of his. We grew up together.

When Alex asked me out on our first date, he checked all the boxes for me. He was wonderful. He was kind. He was smart. He was athletic. He loved the Lord. He was a great man, a great guy. And he had a smile that just made my stomach flip in the best way. It didn't take long before he was my absolute best friend. I could talk to him about anything. He was my first serious boyfriend, and I was his first serious girlfriend. We learned what it meant to fall in love together, navigating all those tricky feelings and learning how to communicate and manage expectations. I couldn't have asked for a better person to figure out love with.

After Alex graduated from college, he had plans to become an actor and model. He started going to auditions, but there isn't exactly the biggest market for that in Nashville. He never complained or talked about how much easier it would be if he moved to Los Angeles or New York. My career was starting to take off, and as a supportive and loving boyfriend, he did his best to make his dreams fit into my life. But by doing that, he wasn't supporting himself.

Alex had built his life around mine at the expense of the things he wanted to achieve. And I had no idea how to make things more equitable. I couldn't pick up and leave Nashville, the literal home of country music and all my hopes and dreams—I had no desire to walk away from my career. We had fights that skirted the issue and discussions that ended in a stalemate because there were no good answers. We both did everything we could to try to make it work. Still, the longer those issues sat unresolved, the more I felt like I was holding him back from being the person he needed to be. I knew deep down that one day he would wake up and resent me for that.

So when Alex got down on one knee and popped the question, I was shocked. I said, "Yes!" How could I say anything else to the man I'd loved with all my heart for the past six years? But that ring came with a growing knot of dread and guilt in the pit of my stomach. I wanted so badly to make it work. I just didn't know how to reconcile all the ways we were growing in different directions. We were very different people at twenty-three than we were at seventeen. When we got engaged, things suddenly got *really real*. Not that it wasn't real before! But when you start planning your entire future and you're not agreeing, those differences begin to carry more weight.

I had a choice: I could marry Alex and get on board with the life he wanted, or I could break his heart and give us both the chance to find the people we were truly right for. I loved him so much that the first option was tempting. I could make Alex happy if I changed enough about myself and ignored my own needs and dreams. But that would mean betraying myself, and I couldn't do that.

I knew I had to be the bad guy, so I ended things.

It was *the worst*. Alex was hurt. I was sad. But ultimately Alex admitted that he had been having doubts too. We hadn't been on the same page for longer than either of us wanted to admit. And beneath the heartbreak, I think we were both relieved.

There were some brutally sad days, but when all was said and done, I knew that he wasn't meant to be my husband. He's no less of a good guy and I'm no less of a good woman for calling it quits.

We all owe it to ourselves to find and fill our lives with the right situations, choices, and people—the right friends, the right coworkers, the right mentors, and hopefully, that one special right person. And if we aren't sure, we have to walk away.

PAINTING THE PICTURE

I used to think that when I became an adult, I'd magically know what all the right decisions were. You have to make *a lot* of choices as an adult, like where to live, which career to pursue, which jobs to take and which to turn down, who to date or marry, what to spend your money on, how to invest your money, who to be friends with, how to function in evolving family dynamics . . . the list goes on and on. For example, I had four different companies to choose between to pick up my trash every week!

Like I said, y'all, *a lot* of choices. All the time.

What I didn't realize as a kid is that most adults are out there making decisions on the fly and just hoping for the best. To some extent, we all have to do that. But the people who are happiest with their choices and their lives are the ones who know themselves and listen to their inner voices. They've taken the time to sift through their desires and dreams to figure out what they really want for the long haul. They have prayed over those plans and know that God wants those things for them too. They aren't sweating the small details or the detours, because they have the big picture firmly in their minds.

> MOST OF US ARE OUT THERE MAKING DECISIONS ON THE FLY AND *HOPING FOR THE BEST.*

Some people have a perfectly clear picture of what they want, and others have a rougher sketch, but the important thing is that they've been able to honestly articulate to themselves what matters most to them. They know that the right people for them won't force them to change that picture. When they meet their closest friends or business partners or the loves of their lives, those people will enhance and add to their dreams, not erase them.

Alex's picture and my picture didn't match. They didn't complement each other. They wouldn't even have made sense hanging next to each other. His picture was beautiful and pure, and it will be the centerpiece of some other girl's heart one day. But as beautiful as it was, I couldn't abandon my picture to live in his—and our pictures didn't mesh together to create a bigger, more beautiful picture. And that's okay. It's good that we realized it before causing each other more pain.

JUST BECAUSE SOMEONE IS A GOOD PERSON, IT DOESN'T MEAN THEY'RE *your* PERSON.

My relationship with Alex taught me that just because someone is a good person, it doesn't mean they're *your* person. I had to break both of our hearts to crack them open so new love could get in. And sometimes that's what you have to do to grow and get to where you need to go. The bottom line is that you can't live for someone else. You have to do the right things for you to create the life you really want.

Get To It

If you don't have a clear picture in your mind of what you want and need in your life, there's no time like the present to start working on that. Start by writing out how you want your life to feel and any words that fit with that.

- Do you want your future to be thrilling, spontaneous, adventurous?
- Calm, cozy, familiar?
- Passionate, active, filled with new challenges?

Take your time. Think about where you might want to live, what you might want your career to be, what your long-term goals and dreams are.

- Do you hope to be married?
- Become a parent?
- Do you have hobbies that are important to you? What are they? Why are they important?

- Are there friends or family you can't imagine being away from (or maybe you can't wait to get away from? Hey, no judgment here!)?

Write it all down. Now it's time to make a visual. We are trying to create a solid mental picture, after all. That picture will help you recognize when you are faced with an opportunity or person that does not fit. A vision board would totally work for this, but instead, I suggest creating a vision book. You can carry it with you and add to your vision as you go. You can even rip out pages if your desires change—and they probably will. The best big pictures are adaptable since you never know what life might throw at you!

Look back at everything you wrote down, and start to make sections in your notebook. You may need to add or delete some of these, but here are some solid areas to help you get started:

- Career
- School
- Family

- Relationships
- Finances
- Travel
- Lifestyle
- Goals
- Religion
- Big Picture

Add the words you already wrote down to the sections they belong in. Then grab a stack of magazines and start looking for images that make you think of those words. Cut those images out and glue them into the notebook.

Over time, your vision book will become more cohesive and begin to make a very personal kind of sense to you. Certain things will keep drawing your eye and heart over and over. Those things are what will make up your big picture. Write them down in your Big Picture section. Move pictures to that section. Keep going until you have a clear idea of what you really want, so you can go after it with everything you've got.

If you already have a pretty good sense of

what you want and where you are going, your big picture might not change much, but it will serve as an excellent reminder of what matters to you and keep you inspired on your worst days.

You deserve to live out that big picture, to get to do all the things that matter most to you. When you know yourself well enough to know what those things are, it's easier to love and value yourself enough to be the bad guy when you have to be and to always be the good guy for yourself.

CHAPTER 6

What Do You Think Of?

LISTENING TO YOUR INSTINCTS TO PROTECT YOURSELF

Have you ever been in a romantic relationship that made you feel like you'd lost your grip on reality? One that was all-consuming and wonderful . . . until it wasn't? And then it felt impossible to get over? A relationship that left your heart so broken and battered that you weren't sure if you'd recover? You're not alone.

The guy who broke my heart was charming and funny, goofy and easy to talk to, earnest and sincere (or at least that's what I thought in the beginning). We'd been friends for a long time, so the transition to something more was easy and natural. Of course, making a relationship last is never as easy as falling for each other.

As smitten as I was, I can see now that a few red flags even then signaled that we wouldn't last. I felt a lot of pressure to fit in with his friends, to change myself to be the woman he wanted. At first, he seemed to love me exactly as I was, but it didn't take long before he began asking me to change in little ways—and then, later, in much bigger ways. I was sometimes baffled by his actions and choices. He'd disappear for days at a time and then suddenly be back as if nothing odd had happened. I blamed it on our busy schedules at first, but then it started happening even when we weren't busy. He'd be distant and dismissive, short tempered over little things. I almost broke it off a few times, but he'd apologize and go back to model boyfriend behavior.

I kept blaming myself for his odd behavior. I couldn't

> MAKING A RELATIONSHIP *LAST* IS NEVER AS EASY AS *FALLING* FOR EACH OTHER.

understand why he was withdrawing, being secretive, and giving me the run-around when I hadn't done anything wrong. He wasn't treating me the way I deserved to be treated. But I loved him, so I kept making excuses for him. I thought maybe I needed to be more understanding, more patient. Maybe if I was the best girlfriend ever, he might change. But no matter how hard I tried, something about how our relationship was progressing didn't feel safe. I just couldn't pinpoint what it was. I was on edge all the time, walking on eggshells with everything I did.

He was also unbearably weird about his phone. I would *never* go through someone's phone, but he was so protective and nervous about his phone that it made me suspicious. It was such extreme behavior that I contemplated sneaking a peek even though I'd never done that to a boyfriend before (or since).

> IF YOU JUST CAN'T SHAKE A FEELING, PLEASE LISTEN TO THAT. *Trust your Gut.*

Of course he was secretive about his phone—he was cheating on me and all the evidence was there! Deep down, I *knew* he wasn't being faithful. I didn't want to believe it, didn't want to see it, but in my heart of hearts, I knew. If you just can't shake a feeling, please listen to that. Trust your gut.

WHEN YOU'RE NOT THE BAD GUY

I wanted so badly to make things work that I did not set boundaries like I should have. I learned so much from this experience and will trust myself if I see similar red flags in the future. If you're in a relationship that feels unsafe, there's a reason. Pay attention! I felt unsafe and uncertain because he was lying to me, treating me badly, sneaking around, and then working very hard to make me feel like it was *my* fault that he was behaving the way he was.

I had never heard the term *gaslighting*, but that's what was happening to me in this relationship. *Gaslighting* is when one person makes the other doubt their own senses and memory. I'd bring up something we'd done or something he'd said, and he'd convince me it had never happened or that I was remembering it wrong. When I got angry about something straightforward, like him lying or ignoring me, he'd turn it around and convince me *I* was the one who'd done something wrong, and before I knew it, I was the one apologizing! It made me feel like I was slowly losing my mind, like there was something wrong with me.

And that made it so difficult to see my situation clearly.

My instincts told me to run, but my heart kept telling me to stay. I finally clawed my way out, but it took much longer than it should have. I should have trusted my instincts when they warned me of danger ahead. I should have heeded the alarm bells that were ringing in my head when he made me question my own memory and sanity.

Maybe you've experienced something similar. If your partner does any of these things, it's *absolutely time* to reassess your relationship:

- consistently lies to you (or others)
- always seems nervous
- criticizes you often and without reason
- is aggressively jealous or territorial
- is controlling
- flirts openly with other women in front of you but acts like you're crazy for calling it out
- tries to limit your contact with friends or family
- always blames other people (or you) for his problems
- is hypersensitive or easily offended
- switches between super charming and super difficult
- has unrealistic expectations of you and others

- is dismissive or contemptuous of your needs and feelings
- refuses to share what he has been doing, even if it affects you
- acts like normal girlfriend behavior is too much or, alternately, not enough (you call too much, you aren't affectionate enough, you expect too much, you don't give him enough of your time, and so on)

All of these behaviors are huge warning signs, especially if your partner is doing some or all of these things and frequently. I'm not talking about if your boyfriend gets jealous once and then apologizes and never does it again. But if he is jealous of every other man you talk to, including *your brother*, it's time to get some help.

If you recognize one or more of the behaviors on that list, take the time to honestly check in with yourself and examine whether your relationship is actually healthy for you. Please don't feel ashamed if your stomach dropped because it sounds *just like* your boyfriend. You aren't alone! I let that guy exhibit almost every single behavior on that list and stayed anyway—for far too long. It happens to more of us than you might think, and there is no shame in admitting you need help. I am so grateful that the support and encouragement of my family and friends helped me finally end things with him.

NO SHAME

I'm sharing this with you—despite how embarrassed I still feel about how badly I let him treat me—because I think it's really important to drag this dark stuff out into the light so we can learn from each other. I was a successful woman who had faced some seriously tough stuff when I met this guy. I had been *through* some stuff. I was confident that if someone treated me badly, I'd just walk away.

But when I was in the thick of it, it wasn't so clear. He went from model boyfriend to needs-to-be-dumped so slowly that I didn't see his behavior for what it was. He gained my trust before he started manipulating me, and he was subtle about it. I want you to know that this can happen to anyone! But it's much less likely to happen to you if you're equipped and go into each relationship with your eyes wide open for warning signs.

Here's the thing: With most guys who exhibit these

IT'S REALLY IMPORTANT TO *DRAG THIS DARK STUFF OUT INTO THE LIGHT* SO WE CAN LEARN FROM EACH OTHER.

types of behaviors, things start out great. They are charming and intense and make you feel special and wonderful. So of course, when things aren't so wonderful anymore, you believe that you can get back to that good place if you just cater to his demands or become more invested in the relationship. But you'll never get back to that good place—because the good stuff was a lie, an act he put on to hook you. Still, those happy memories can make it difficult to see a way out.

WORKING THROUGH
THE HEARTBREAK

When my relationship finally fell apart, it should have been a relief, right? I should have been celebrating that I'd dodged a bullet! Instead, I was crushed. I threw myself into work, but distracting myself from the pain didn't make the pain go away. My heart was still broken. I don't know about you, but I can't just turn off love for someone, no matter how badly they hurt me. I talked my friends' ears off, debating whether or not we should get back together, wondering if I'd made a mistake by not staying. I cried enough tears for a lifetime. I questioned my choices, even though I knew deep down that I had done the right thing.

But slowly and steadily, the fog began to lift, and I could see my situation for what it was.

Of course, it wasn't a clean break. It very rarely is with this type of relationship. He called me a lot. He wanted to get back together. I still loved him, so this was really painful and difficult—but I told him not to call me anymore. I set a boundary, and man, was that hard! I had finally realized that I deserved better and that he would never be able to give me better.

You've probably heard the saying that when someone shows you who they are, believe them. I really loved this guy and was good to him, but he did *not* treat me well. He was showing me who he was. When someone doesn't give back the love and consideration you're giving, you begin to question yourself. *What's wrong with me? Why am I not enough?* Please know that their behavior is about *them*, not about you.

As sad and hurt as I was, I couldn't continue to be angry at him for not being who I wanted and needed him to be. Carrying that kind of anger only hurts you in the long run. I knew who he was, and more importantly, I knew myself well enough to be certain that he wasn't the guy for me. Loving him wouldn't change that. Being angry at him wouldn't change that. Hating him wouldn't change that either.

All I could do was let him go, set boundaries to protect myself, and begin to heal.

So I did.

Over the course of your life, you'll meet a lot of possible romantic partners. Some of them will be for you. Some won't. And like me, you may end up in some situations that break your heart. But those moments also provide opportunity for big growth! When you know yourself well, it's much easier to tell the difference at the outset—and much easier to let go of the wrong guys. It's okay to give people the benefit of the doubt, to give people chances. People do mess up, see the error of their ways, and make amends. I'm not saying you need to walk away at the first sign of trouble. I *am* saying to decide how you want to be treated by people in your life and *hold that line*—because you deserve to be treated well. When someone consistently crosses that line, it's time to walk away.

> DECIDE HOW YOU WANT TO BE TREATED AND *HOLD THAT LINE*—BECAUSE YOU DESERVE TO BE TREATED WELL.

We'll come across people who won't treat us the way

they should, but it doesn't have to break us. Before you find the person you're meant to be with forever, you'll probably come across a number of possibilities. Some may love you . . . some might not. But the most important person who will ever love you is *you*. So keep working to encourage yourself and lift yourself up, and never let go of the commitment to yourself that you *deserve* to be loved well. And then don't settle for anything less.

Get To It

The middle of a rocky relationship is not the ideal time to figure out what you really want out of it. The best, most loving thing you can do for yourself when it comes to relationships is to define, for yourself, what a healthy relationship looks like *before* you're in one.

Figure out now what your deal breakers are. Someone who lies is one of mine. So is cheating, not communicating consistently, flaking on plans, or name-calling during fights. Think about how your dream person would treat you.

- How would they make you feel?
- How would they speak to you?
- How would they handle disagreements?
- How would they respond in a crisis?

Your deal breakers should be fair, consistent, and realistic and ones you would expect your partner to have too. It's difficult to hold someone to a standard that you aren't willing and able to meet yourself. There is no perfect person. Every relationship will have disagreements, hiccups, and misunderstandings. It's important to find people who can handle those things with respect and compassion.

Once you have your deal breakers in mind, look at your current or past relationship. Did any cross the line? If you're in a relationship right now, is it within those boundaries you've defined?

Perhaps you haven't communicated your expectations clearly. Start now and get really honest. Let this person know what you expect from them and what you expect from yourself. Then follow through.

It may take time to get used to the new boundaries you're setting, so give extra grace. It will become clear quickly if this person is for you. They won't have issues with respecting your boundaries and honestly probably won't have to change much about how they treat you. It will also become clear if this person isn't right. Anyone who pitches a fit about you setting boundaries isn't likely to respect them and probably doesn't really respect you.

It hurts to let go of someone! Even if they're toxic and aren't good for you, that doesn't mean your heart won't hurt. But please know that you can't change anyone but yourself. No matter how much you love someone, how much you give, how much you hope and pray, he won't change unless *he* wants to. So when someone isn't who you want them to be, the only thing you can change is how you respond.

I know that's easier said than done. Clearly it was a process for me. Take it day by day and accept the accompanying emotions. The most helpful thing I know to do with my emotions is write about them. After we broke up, I wrote song after song. I think I covered all the emotions—anger, sadness, betrayal, and ultimately, gratitude. And I truly *was* grateful. As painful as that relationship was, it also taught me that I can be strong and set boundaries and that I can choose to love myself and treat myself well even when someone I love doesn't do the same.

You don't have to write music. You can write poetry or a memoir or in a journal. You can paint or sing or go for long walks or knit or bake cupcakes—whatever helps get your feelings out. It really helps to just get the words out of your head! I wrote an entire short collection of break-up songs. (Shameless plug! If you need a soundtrack to help heal your broken heart, check out *Getting Over Him*.) Find a familiar, comforting activity to help you channel your sadness into something creative. You never know, you might create something beautiful.

The other helpful thing for me was to take

control and start a new chapter of my story that I was excited about. I pushed myself to try something new during that time, and it helped keep my focus off my heartache. If you find yourself with a broken heart, it's good to find focus with new projects and goals you're excited about. Take a dance class with your best friends, order that calligraphy notebook you've been eyeing, plant a garden, or launch that side hustle. Take on something challenging that will enrich your story, and shift your focus away from who you lost and back to who you gained—yourself.

CHAPTER 7

Talking to God

LEARNING TO TRUST GOD IN THE GOOD TIMES AND THE BAD TIMES

I want to share something that I think we all forget about sometimes: God is there for you.

No matter how you are feeling or what you are dealing with or how messy and hopeless your life is at the moment, God is right there. So why does it always seem like we wait until we are desperate to reach out and talk to Him?

I don't think we forget about God or somehow believe we don't need Him. I always *know* I need God. But I think a lot of people hesitate to reach out to God because of shame. We don't feel like we deserve God's love or His help. We are painfully aware of all the ways we don't measure up to the ideal of a "good Christian," all the ways we've messed up or failed. I know I've felt that way—ashamed and down on myself and feeling like way too much of a holy hot mess to talk to God about anything.

> GOD KNOWS THAT WE'RE ALL ON THE *HOT mess express* AND LOVES US ANYWAY.

But that doesn't mean God sees me like that! Or maybe God just knows that we're all on the hot mess express and loves us anyway. If God can love us just as we are, doesn't it make sense that we should love ourselves like that too?

WE DON'T HAVE TO DO IT ALONE

When life gets rough and rocky, it's time to admit that going it alone is not working and that we need God. Sometimes we realize this on our own; sometimes life forces the realization. And let me tell you: we definitely need God *way* more than we need to keep hiding in our shame.

That's when it's time to hit our knees and start praying. And that's always when I'm so thankful that God isn't a person like you or me. Because if someone I loved (the way God loves us) ignored me when I tried to help and made self-destructive choices and then tried to hide all of it from me—all while saying we were still friends—well, I might not be so willing to jump in and help when they finally admitted they needed me.

But God doesn't keep score like we do. He's watched too many of us go through the same cycle over and over since literally *the beginning of time*. He knows how humans operate, and He forgives us every single time. That is some serious love, huh?

WHEN EVERYTHING GOES WRONG

My faith was really clarified and defined in the year when it felt like everything went wrong. My parents divorced. My dad went through rehab. My mother remarried. My eating disorder came to light, and I struggled so much to overcome it. I had to have vocal cord surgery (I wasn't even sure if I'd be able to sing again).

In addition to all of that, I'd just moved to Nashville and felt so far away from my family and friends. My career was faltering, and I was broke. And I do mean *broke*. I was so far down that I finally had to look up. And I found God waiting for me.

I had instant fame but not instant success. You have to work for success and put in the time. Competing on *American Idol* made me famous, but it didn't automatically earn me a top spot on the country charts. I got my fame on a show that had produced only a few superstars. I needed to prove that I had the talent and the chops to make it on my own.

American Idol was a *high* high, so it makes sense that the low that followed was a *low* low. I had a lot of misses on country radio. The manager I mentioned earlier not only broke me down; she also left me broke.

So when I finally fired that manager, I found myself living in an apartment in Franklin that I definitely could not afford. I was so hard up for cash that I sold the cherry red Shelby Mustang Cobra I'd won on *American Idol* just to make it another few months. I waited until I really had no other choice, because that car was like my trophy for

American Idol, the one tangible thing I had to remember my time there. I was devastated to let the car go, but desperate times call for desperate measures. So I paid the rent for a while with that money, but I was still on a tight budget (fun fact: my family bought that car back for me later!).

My budget was so tight that I couldn't even afford groceries some weeks. Around that time, I signed a contract with my current manager, Trisha. She was a total godsend and really changed my life. One of the first things she did was loan me ten thousand dollars (it was such a proud day when I paid that back!). And just before that money ran out, she landed me a deal with Cracker Barrel. They paid me in these gold meal cards they were promoting at the time. God was looking out for me that day, I'll tell you what. It was too perfect that those cards were gold because they were literally like pieces of gold to me. If I hadn't had those, there would've been days when I couldn't afford to eat at all. I basically ate at Cracker Barrel around the clock for months. You can bet your biscuits that I said a heartfelt prayer of thanks every time I walked through that Old Country Store.

I'm sure the staff at Cracker Barrel wondered about the girl who came in three times a day, but I didn't care if people thought I was weird. I was too grateful. My go-to order was the grilled chicken dinner plate with a house salad with ranch dressing, mashed potatoes (or the hash-brown casserole, personal fave!), and the mac and cheese. And of course, biscuits. I never skimped on those! I was so thankful for those biscuits. I'd usually take a box to go for a snack for later.

GRACE BIGGER THAN BISCUITS

That was a really lonely time for me. You can spend only so many evenings with your to-go biscuits before you start to wish you had some friends. I was eighteen when I moved to Nashville. I didn't know where to meet people, because most people my age were in college. I was too young to go to bars but too old to hang with high schoolers, so it was tough to find friends. Alex was going to college in Murfreesboro, which is fairly close to Franklin. It helped to have him nearby, and I made some friends through him, but they weren't close, tell-each-other-all-your-secrets friends. They were more like watch-a-game-and-grab-pizza friends. You can always grab pizza with your secret-telling friends, but you can't tell secrets to your pizza-grabbing friends, you know?

My faith is an important part of my day-to-day life now, but it wasn't always that way. I'd been more of an only-think-about-God-in-church-on-Sundays girl for years. It wasn't that I didn't believe (I did!) or that I didn't love God (I did!). It was just that God felt distant to me, not like someone who would be concerned with my small problems. I always just felt like He had bigger fish to fry, like helping widows and orphans and addressing world hunger. You know, more serious stuff. I couldn't imagine that He really cared about why I wanted to lose ten pounds or my meeting with my record label.

Even on my worst days, I knew I had it better than *so* many people. I didn't need God to rain down love and grace on me like those other people did, right?

Wrong. I needed that so, so, so much.

I just didn't feel like I deserved it. And I didn't. None of us do! But God can't wait to shower us with His love and grace and hope and joy anyway. I was treating God like a person again, assuming that He has limits on His time and power—when those limits do not exist. God can love me and care deeply about my life while simultaneously loving and caring deeply about every other person on this planet. I was assuming that God has only so much love and grace to give before He gets tired or runs out.

Which is silly—because He *is* love and grace. He will never run out.

Around that time is when I really started spending time with the Lord. I prayed and prayed and prayed that year (while being grateful for those to-go biscuits). Talking to God helped keep me afloat. I'm thankful for this hard season because it brought me closer to Him, but we don't necessarily have to go through tough times to grow closer to God. Because He's always there and He's always providing good things. When we're down, it can be so easy to focus on all the stuff that's going wrong and spend all of our time complaining to God or begging for big changes.

I can see now what I couldn't see back then: God was answering my prayers, every single one of them. He just wasn't answering them as fast as I wanted or even in the exact ways I thought were best.

Turns out that His timing is *way* better than what I had in mind.

He brought me amazing secret-telling friends, one at a time, giving me the space to get to know each woman and cement our bond before bringing another friend my way. The women I became friends with that year are still some of my best, most trusted friends, and I am so grateful for them. I probably wouldn't have met any of them if

WE DON'T HAVE TO
GO THROUGH TOUGH
TIMES TO GROW
CLOSER TO GOD.
He's ALWAYS THERE.

I hadn't been pushed out of my comfort zone and forced to try some new things. God made sure I had something I could sell for rent money. He gave me daily bread—well, biscuits—when I couldn't afford anything else.

And ultimately, He helped me top the charts—but only when I was ready to handle the success, when I had found healthy ways to work on the issues that would have sabotaged me and held me back. He was stacking my deck, but I didn't understand that until I finally saw the whole hand.

A WINNING HAND

If I'd been successful right out of the gate post–*American Idol*, I don't think I'd appreciate everything I have nearly as much as I do now. I know what it's like to be hungry, to live month to month going after your dream, always dreading a bounced check. I know what it's like to have songs flop, to be told no and get passed over for tours and opportunities. I know how gut-wrenching it is to not book the gig when that paycheck would have made the biggest difference. I know those feelings intimately, so you can bet I don't take what I have for granted.

God knows our strengths and weaknesses. He knows what we need to learn, and He helps to make sure we learn it—even if it's painful and even if we've been ignoring Him. I owe my success to Him, not just with my music but in all areas of my life.

> GOD KNOWS WHAT WE NEED TO LEARN—EVEN IF IT'S *PAINFUL* AND EVEN IF WE'VE BEEN *IGNORING HIM*.

Maybe you're reading this and thinking, *Listen, I read my Bible every day and twice on Sundays.* Or maybe you wouldn't touch a Bible with a ten-foot pole. Either way, you're welcome here with me. But I couldn't write this book without telling you all about what God has done for me, and I want that same divine freedom for every person I meet.

God has taught me so much, loved me so much, and given me all I have, at every step. I want you to know that God loves you too with the unconditional, all-encompassing love we are all searching for. He's got so much to show you, to teach you, to give you.

All you have to do is start talking.

Get To It

When I started talking to God regularly instead of only when things were at their worst, it opened my eyes and heart in so many different ways. I saw more clearly all the ways God was working things for my good—even when it didn't always make sense at the time. I felt more thankful for the challenges I faced because I could see how they were shaping and teaching me, preparing me for the amazing things God has in store for me.

The more I've grown to love myself, the more I've been able to accept God's love for me—and not just accept it but savor it. Instead of waiting until I'm desperate, I talk to God every day. I think it's like any other relationship. You have to feed it regularly to keep it strong. I thank Him and praise Him, like I was taught in church, but I also just hang out with Him. I know I can confide all my thoughts and emotions to Him. I talk to God about how I'm feeling and what I've been thinking about. What I'm worried about and what I'm encouraged by.

What I'm dreaming about for myself and for the world in general. What is bringing me joy and what is weighing me down. I even share my puns with Him. I like to think they make Him chuckle too.

- What are you talking to God about?
- What are you *not* talking to God about?
- What are you trying to handle on your own?
- What are some good things in your life you could share with God?

When I can't find the words to talk to God, I sing to Him instead. I sing worship songs, hymns, new music I'm working on, and old favorites. My voice and my love of music are both gifts that God gave me. Since He gave them to me, I know that He must delight in them. You have abilities and passions that are gifts from God too, special things that are only yours that He delights in. Do you know what those things are? Take a minute to jot down all of the gifts and passions you've been blessed with.

God gave us all gifts for a reason, and He expects us to use them. Even at the point when I had the least amount of self-confidence, I always knew I could go out on stage and sing and feel fulfilled and perfectly made. In those moments, I always felt God's love so deeply that I was able to borrow a little of it for myself. If you're struggling to find that special gift God gave you, think through the things you enjoy.

- Is there something that feels easier than other pursuits or activities?
- Where do you get in the zone and feel energized?
- Is there any particular activity that makes you feel truly alive?

That may be just the thing God is calling you to do.

CHAPTER 8

The Other Side

CLIMBING THE MOUNTAIN OF GRIEF

Loss is a part of life. But I believe we'll see those we love again. I truly believe that we will be reunited with them in heaven. I may still be young, but I've lost quite a few people I loved over the years. That sense of loss and grief never really goes away. It gets easier to carry, more muted and less urgent with time, but it never fully disappears. Each loss is still imprinted on my heart today. And that's just fine with me. The love of these people helped shape me and make me the woman I am today. I'm proud to carry a little piece of each of them with me, even if it's tinged with grief.

The loss that affected me the most deeply was the death of Sam, my stepfather. Sam was the most positive, upbeat, uplifting person you'd ever met. He was always smiling, always happy in every situation. He radiated positivity—always. The only times I ever saw him cry were big moments for my brother and me. His life was a great example of the kind of person I want to be and how to behave and carry myself to be the kind of woman that would make him proud. He was a man of honor and integrity, and his word was as good as gold. He brought so much love and healing to our family when he married my mom. He was so inspiring, just truly the best guy ever.

It was such a shock when we found out Sam was sick. He was always the healthiest and most upbeat person in our family. He had been in the Marine Corps and was in great shape physically. He ran six miles a day. He ate well. You never would've expected Sam to get sick.

But Sam wasn't just a little sick. He had stage four melanoma.

By the time the doctors found it, the cancer was in his spine and had already spread to both of his lungs and his liver. It was all over the place. Even though the doctors said his prognosis wasn't good, I really thought he had a good chance of beating it—because *he* was so positive he could beat it. Sam never once complained. He was so full of faith the entire time. "I'm going to be healed. I'm gonna beat it." I mean, he said this a million times, and he always smiled. He never felt sorry for himself.

Sam fought really, really hard. I prayed so much, just begging and pleading with God to save Sam. For a while, I had so much hope. I really wanted this miracle. My family *needed* this miracle. We were prayer warriors. And Sam believed, more firmly than anyone, that he would be healed. But the initial treatment didn't work. So next we tried a clinical trial out in California, but that didn't work either. They sent him home on hospice care. We set up his bed and medical equipment in the living room so as many of us as possible could be with him around the clock. I think that's when I realized no miracle was coming and I got angry.

WHEN THE MIRACLE DOESN'T COME

Grief is such a weird thing and there are so many stages of grief, but I always seem to get stalled out for a long time in the anger phase. In the last month or so of Sam's life, I questioned everything about my faith. I even wondered

if maybe we'd made up this whole God thing because He sure didn't seem to be listening.

I just didn't understand how someone like Sam, who was so prayerful and so hopeful and so faithful, could be dying. I was so stuck in my own sadness that I couldn't even feel God anymore. He was right there beside me, but I let my grief drown out all of the comfort and peace He was holding out to me.

A few weeks before Sam died, I told God, "I know You're real and I know You're out there, but You don't seem to be listening. And when he dies, I'm never talking to You again." Like I said, I was really, really, really angry to be losing Sam.

I'm so thankful God didn't hold that time or my anger against me. Instead, He reached out in the midst of my grief and gave me the most incredible gift I could have ever asked for.

My family was all together with Sam at the end. All we could do was sit and wait and try to manage Sam's pain. He hadn't spoken in a few days, and the nurses told us that he might not speak again. It was so difficult for all of us to watch him suffer and decline.

All of a sudden, Sam opened his eyes and said very clearly, "I found it."

He wasn't looking at us, he was looking straight up at the ceiling and seeing something we couldn't see. My mom, holding his hand, said, "What did you find, Sam?"

"Heaven," he said. "I wish you could see it."

In that moment, we could see Sam's body relax, as if every ounce of pain had been washed away. He looked so at peace. And you could feel the peace in the room too. It was unbelievable. A room that, just moments before, had been practically suffocating under the weight of our grief, sadness, anger, and confusion was suddenly the most peaceful place I've ever been. It gives me chills just thinking about it.

For the next few minutes Sam told us about heaven. He said he saw Jesus, who was beautiful. And he saw his mama, who'd been gone for many years, running toward him, looking young and happy, just like she had been when he was a kid. His voice was so filled with awe and joy, and he was so excited to see everyone who was waiting for him there.

And then Sam said, "I love you all, but I have to go now," and closed his eyes.

A few hours later, Sam left us for somewhere far better.

WHEN THE HEALING LOOKS DIFFERENT

Can you imagine how I felt, sitting there listening to Sam? I had just told God that I would never speak to Him again, and here He was showing us a glimpse of heaven through my stepfather's final few hours.

It's difficult to put into words what we experienced in that room, the peace and comfort that none of us could have possibly felt without Jesus. I think we got a glimpse of what is described in Revelation 21:4: "He will wipe every tear from their eyes. There will be no more death or mourning or crying or pain, for the old order of things has passed away."

That day changed my life forever. We got a glimpse of what it will be like someday without grief, when all that will remain is God's peace and joy and hope. Honestly, I'll never forget those moments and that feeling as long as I live. The look on Sam's face was so reverent and held such pure, radiant joy. Sam had been so sick, in so much pain, and it was just gone in those moments. It was *all* gone as he literally *described* heaven to us.

That miracle we all prayed for? For healing? We got it.

God healed Sam completely when He brought him home.

And He healed me too. I still had plenty more healing to do, but God stopped the bleeding in my heart created by anger, grief, and a lack of faith.

Those moments with Sam singlehandedly deepened my faith more than anything else that has ever happened to me. I don't think I could ever question God's existence or His goodness again after experiencing that. The peace my family felt was the biggest and most generous gift God could have given in a time when we so desperately needed it.

Death can feel like a hopeless thing, but it can be full of hope if we know the truth that we will see one another again someday. I truly believe that God is real, that Jesus is real, and that they are waiting for us in heaven. We will be reunited with our loved ones who have passed. I know because I witnessed it. I saw Sam's eyes light up and say, "Mom!" when he saw his mother. And that's exactly how excited I will be when I get to see him again.

LOVE IS NEVER LOST

I think the most important thing we can do is love one another, lift each other up, and hold tight to the knowledge that someday we're all going to be reunited in heaven. My mom tells my nephews, "He's just up there building our mansion," which always makes me smile. I'm not really sure how the whole heaven thing works, but if you are allowed to build a mansion, then I'm sure that's what he's doing. I'm going to see my stepdad again.

It's comforting to know that Sam is waiting for us in heaven, but that doesn't mean the pain of losing him has magically vanished. His loss will stay with me forever. He's been gone for a few years now, and there are still days when my grief overwhelms me out of nowhere. I've had to learn to lean into the grief on those days. If I can, I clear my schedule, put on my coziest sweats, pick up some serious comfort food (chicken tenders and mac 'n' cheese, anyone?), and spend the day looking through old pictures or watching sad movies. It's okay to embrace comfort, whatever that means to you, to help you through.

I've also had to really mentally prepare for big days when Sam's absence feels more overpowering than anyone else's presence. Christmas morning, Thanksgiving dinner, and Easter Sunday have all been tinged with loss. Nights when I've been up for an award or giving a big performance are harder than I expected. I can't help but look for Sam's calming, proud presence and miss it desperately. I doubt I'll ever stop missing him on those days, but I know that he wouldn't want me to be sad. He'd be the first one trying to cheer me up and encouraging me to find the good despite my grief. He'd want me to celebrate his legacy. Knowing that helps me to choose joy instead of letting myself get too stuck in despair.

I really feel compelled to tell Sam's story because I know that many of us have lost people—and may have lost our faith and hope in the process. I know that a lot of families don't get that explicit reassurance from God that we did. I know that so many of us spend years and years questioning God and His love. And it's not just death that causes loss. We can grieve so many things. The former best friend who disappeared and we don't know why. The guy you thought was "the one" who broke your heart. A tightly held dream that fell to pieces in front of you. A life-altering opportunity that changed your life in all the wrong ways. A medical diagnosis that leaves you missing your former freedom.

Any loss can be devastating. And I know that so many of us carry grief in our hearts daily, wounds that never seem to heal. That may be where you are right now. If it is, I'm so sorry.

When we're dealing with overwhelming pain, it can feel safer to curl in on ourselves and block everyone else out, and that includes God. We don't want to have to explain our grief, and we can't imagine that anyone else could understand the depth of the loss we're dealing with. We think we need to be alone to mourn, but in the process, we block out the compassion and comfort of those who love us. And even worse, we lock the pain inside ourselves, making it almost impossible to find healing.

Others do understand. Loss is a part of life. Almost everyone you know has lost someone or something they loved dearly. I promise that you know people who have been where you are right now. You just need to give them a chance to help. They won't try to minimize your pain, and they won't try to force you to be okay when you aren't.

IT'S NOT JUST DEATH THAT *causes loss.*

And God? Well, He understands far better than anyone else. He had to watch and feel it all when His Son, Jesus, died on the cross. He chose to feel that pain and grief to save you and me. He's been there. He knows loss intimately. He understands, and He's big enough and powerful enough to hold you and your pain and anger and denial and sadness. God can handle it if you need to be mad at Him. He's not going anywhere, and He's waiting for you right now, regardless of how long it's been, to start healing your heart with His love.

Loss will never be easy. There is no time line for when you should feel better or when you should be "over it." In fact, it's 100 percent okay if you're never really over it. But hopefully, you can lean on God until your heart is less tender and you're able to see the beauty still waiting for you in the world. You'll know when you're ready to get back out there and start writing your story again.

GOD CAN HANDLe iT IF YOU NEED TO BE MAD AT HIM.

Just remember that love is never lost. The love of the ones you lost will become part of the love you have for yourself and others. And someday, you'll be able to share that story with those you love when you finally see them again on the other side.

Get To It

The thing about losing someone you love is that it's over for them. They're in heaven rejoicing. Or in the case of relationships that ended in other ways, they are off living their life without you. But the difficulties are just beginning for those of us still here, mourning their loss. We have to figure out how to go on without them. If that's what you're facing right now, there are steps you can take to make that process easier (these steps really helped me!).

- *Shake things up.* If old routines and habits keep pulling you back down into your grief, change them. Identify the things that trigger the worst of your grief, and make some swaps. Instead of eating breakfast alone at the table you used to share, grab a muffin and go for a walk in the fresh air.
- *Talk to God.* Pray. Pour your feelings out to God and let Him help you carry the weight.
- *Get help.* There is no right or wrong way to process loss, and there is no time line for grief. You have to find what feels right for you. But if you're feeling

really overwhelmed and lost, it's absolutely okay to ask for help. Seek out a grief support group, ask your friends for extra support, or find a therapist to talk to. There are no gold medals for going it alone.

- *Invest in yourself.* Spend some money if you're able to access resources that will help you. Book some therapy appointments. Rent a little spot by the beach or in the mountains for a soothing getaway. Sign up for lessons or take on a new hobby to give you something fun to look forward to and be excited about.
- *Be realistic with your expectations.* Mentally prepare yourself for big days and holidays, occasions that will be happy. You'll need to accept the fact that there will be sadness on those days that wasn't there before. You will also need to accept that it's still okay to be happy on those days. In fact, your loved ones would want you to be. It might

help to have a phrase you can repeat to yourself for comfort, such as, "It's okay to be sad, but it's okay to be happy too. I know my lost loved one would want me to enjoy life."

- *Give yourself grace.* You will have rough days. Make a promise to yourself to be gentle with your heart on those days. You don't have to push through and achieve at your usual levels. Be tender and kind, and don't beat yourself up. You'll get back to full speed eventually, and even if you don't, that doesn't make you any less worthy of grace and love from yourself and the people in your life.

- *Hit pause.* It's okay to take a break from anyone in your life who makes dealing with this loss more difficult: the well-meaning friend who is full of useless platitudes, the relative who wants to keep reminiscing when you aren't ready for that yet, the coworker who keeps asking overly personal questions, or even the parade of friends who want to visit or bring food when you need time alone. Say "thanks, but no thanks" to these people. You aren't obligated to pour your heart out to anyone. Take a break and rekindle these relationships when *you're* ready.

- *Allow yourself time to cry.* If you're fighting to reestablish some control over your emotions, try setting aside time each day to mourn. Use that time to cry and rail and think about your loss as much as you want. Having some allotted time to let your emotions run wild will help you keep them in check at other times when you need to deal with life.

- *Embrace comfort.* Eat that mac 'n' cheese that reminds you of childhood. Snuggle under a blanket and watch old movies all day. Spend the entire weekend in bed reading novels and eating chocolate. Skip nights out to go to bed early, or alternately, go out every night if being around people is soothing to you. While these might not be habits you want to become permanent, a little coziness and indulgence can help aid the healing process.

- *Live the legacy.* Look at your loved one's life. What did you learn from them? How did they help you grow and develop into the person you are today? Celebrate those things and share them with others. In that way, you are helping spread their love and keep their legacy going. And that's a beautiful thing.

Loss will always be part of life. And we all have to face it at some point. The best we can do is to let ourselves mourn and then, when we're ready, pick ourselves up and keep living our lives in a way that would make the people we've loved proud.

CHAPTER 9

HOLDING THE OTHER

IT TAKES A VILLAGE

Picture this. It's CMA Fest, country music's biggest celebration. CMA Music Festival is a huge festival held every year in downtown Nashville dedicated to country music fans. Tens of thousands of fans descend on Nashville for that week.

It's an honor to be asked to perform, and I was thrilled to be singing on the second-biggest stage on that particular day. Unfortunately, things weren't going as planned. I was running behind, which I absolutely hate. Running late makes me really anxious. So as I sat there while my stylist finished my hair and my makeup artist brushed on the fastest smoky eye ever, I was getting super nervous that I would miss my performance time. As soon as my glam squad finished, I got dressed and was out the door.

During CMA Fest, all the streets in the main downtown area of Nashville are blocked off so fans can walk the streets and get around more easily. Normally I love that, but on this day, all I wanted was a direct route to the Riverfront Stage, which, as you may have gathered by the name, is on the bank of the river just past First Avenue. My manager, Trisha, drove my assistant at the time, Eden, and me down as far as she could until she hit the roadblocks at 8th Avenue and Demonbreun. It was still a long, long way to the river. We jumped out with all of our bags and took off running, hair blowing in the wind, as we pushed through the huge crowds.

We must have been quite the sight! I was wearing my full stage get-up—a sparkly jumpsuit and killer high heels—and I was hustling with everything I had in me. Eden was running behind me dragging a massive rolling suitcase, and that sucker was heavy! Despite all of that,

Eden managed to yell and flag down a golf cart. I jumped on the golf cart while Eden was throwing on the bags. Then the driver took off before Eden could get on. I wasn't about to leave Eden behind, so I grabbed her hand and yanked her on just in time. I have to give some serious credit to the lady driving that golf cart. She put the pedal to the metal to get me down to the stage.

When we arrived, my sound guy was waiting with my microphone and all the sound equipment I needed to wear on stage. He pulled me over to a barely covered area so Eden could hook on my sound pack. Let me tell you, you don't want to have your jumpsuit unzipped down the back in the middle of downtown Nashville on a busy day! We were covered, but I felt so exposed! Thankfully Trisha had called ahead, and my band had completed the sound check for me. Everyone had stepped up to cover the things I normally would have handled.

There was no time to fix my hair or adjust anything. I literally ran up onto the stage, still out of breath from my sprint down Demonbreun, just in time to start the performance. I never would have made it and been there singing for my fans if my entire team hadn't pulled together so well. From my makeup artist, who made me gorgeous in record time, to Trisha driving and coordinating everything behind the scenes, to Eden sprinting down the street with all of my stuff, to our NASCAR-ready golf cart driver, to my team meeting us next to the stage to get everything ready, to my band making it work on the fly—well, that day we were the definition of "teamwork makes the dream work."

IN THIS TOGETHER

No one achieves anything in this world alone. No matter how smart or talented or wonderful you are, the honest truth is that you need other people to help you, to take a chance on you, to believe in you, support you, and cheer you on. I may be the one on stage performing or accepting an award, but I share those moments with everyone who helped get me up there—my family, my friends, my manager, my songwriting partners, my producers, my band and road crew, the session musicians who played on my tracks, everyone at my record label, my PR team, my agency, my hair and makeup artists, my stylists, my assistant, my management coordinator, and the list goes on and on.

I've been a part of a lot of teams over the years—my Special Olympics teams, softball teams, my cheerleading squad, and now, the Lauren Alaina team—and I can honestly say that I'd rather be on a team anytime than trying to go it alone. Teams can accomplish much more than any one of us can achieve by ourselves, so working alongside other dedicated, talented, passionate people to achieve a big goal is something special. When a team really comes together, it's pretty magical. Being on a team means you have someone to shore up your weakest skills, and your strengths can compensate for someone else's problem spots. Input from so many different people with a variety of backgrounds and experiences allows you to anticipate problems more quickly and to come up with more creative solutions. And truly, there's nothing like the rush of celebrating with your team when you make that goal.

Of course, not all teams wear matching jerseys or work together. The first team I was ever part of was my family. I feel really fortunate I grew up with two involved parents who are still here for me. My mom has always given me the best advice, told me over and over how beautiful and precious I am to her, and she always answers my calls, even in the middle of the night. My father is one of my first calls anytime I'm in need. He was one of the first people to really nurture my love of music. He'd go with me to performances and play his guitar while I sang. He was my very first backup, and he always will be. I am so grateful to have that relationship with my parents.

My team is, of course, bigger than just my parents. My brother and sister-in-law, my adorable nephews, my aunts, uncles, cousins, and grandparents have all been my absolute biggest cheerleaders and fans. I've always been able to count on them to pick me back up when I fall, sing along the loudest at my shows, and love me when I'm feeling low.

As I've already said, I also have an amazing therapist. I know I keep talking about therapy! Go ahead and call me obsessed. But seriously, therapy has been life changing for me! My counselor has helped me discover the tools I desperately needed to deal with my eating disorder and to help me love my body and to see myself with fresh eyes.

I have wonderful friends, truly wonderful. All of my friends hold a different space for me. I do Bible studies with my friend Ainsley. My friends Megan and Katelyn are my church and brunch buddies. Sarah Beth is my friend I know I can tell anything to and she'll never judge me. Molly is more than my assistant. She is my travel companion and partner in crime—I couldn't do life without her. My stylist, Amber, and my makeup artist, Meri, have been with me since the beginning of my career and are like the older sisters I never had. Amber Cannon, my hair stylist, is the newest addition to my glam team and has been the missing puzzle piece that completes our Laurentourage. I also have trusted guy friends—Connor, Jason,

> BEING ON A TEAM ISN'T JUST ABOUT THE BENEFITS YOU RECEIVE; IT'S ALSO ABOUT THE WAYS YOU GET TO *serve your teammates* AND MAKE *THEIR* LIVES BETTER.

and Michael Zuehsow (Zeus for short)—who give me that male perspective when I need it. And I have Trisha, my manager, who is my number-one supporter and holds my hand through everything.

BUILD THAT TEAM FROM THE GROUND UP

Seeing this list, I realize it might sound like I'm bragging—and maybe I am a little. I just feel so lucky to have found these people and am so grateful that they love me. They are all part of the family I've chosen for myself, the team I know I can always count on. I'm so honored to have them and even more honored that I get to be on each of their teams too. Because being on a team isn't just about the benefits you receive; it's also about the ways you get to serve your teammates and make *their* lives better.

Building up these friendships and relationships takes time and energy and a level of vulnerability and commitment that is often a stretch. But you can't build a trustworthy team without actually trusting them. And to be on their teams, I had to be open and honest with them so that they knew they could trust me too.

Once I had community around me I could trust, I started to be more comfortable with opening up. I hadn't realized just how heavy what I was carrying was until someone else took some of that weight. Even if my team doesn't have answers, just the fact that I can talk to them about my problems makes the load lighter. I never want to be a burden, but I know how grateful I am when I can help *them* carry their loads. Why would I think they feel any differently about me? Now I don't hesitate to ask for help when I need it. Knowing I can trust my team to show up for me makes life a lot better.

If you struggle to be vulnerable, start with the person you know is least likely to judge, offer an opinion, or try to suggest changes. Share something small but important. I know you'll feel nervous putting your emotions on display and showing someone the messiness you typically try to hide, but if this person is truly on your team, they'll respond with compassion and encouragement. And probably hugs. Lots of hugs. And if your least judgmental person is like my least judgmental person, Sarah Beth, they will respond with cozy blankets and mac 'n' cheese too.

Life is really hard. It's *guaranteed* that we'll each face issues that we simply cannot handle alone. We can try to muddle our way through a two-person job by ourselves or we can call in a friend for support. We can choose to remain isolated and lonely, or we can let a few trusted people into our mess . . . discover that our mess doesn't seem nearly as bad once we have help. We can choose to let our people love us the way that we love them.

Life takes a village, and we were never meant to go it alone! We are called to care for each other and love one another. We sometimes have to do some work to find our crews, but then the sky's the limit! We get to be totally and completely honest when we're going through stuff and need them. Wouldn't you want the same from your closest loved ones so you can love and cheer for them? Of course! We can fight for them. We can hold their hands through the hard times and through the victories too. We can celebrate together. Have fun. Make each other laugh until our

CHOOSE TO LET YOUR

PEOPLE LOVE YOU

THE WAY YOU

LOVE THEM.

stomachs hurt. Complain and cry together. Be exhausted and overwhelmed together. And find our grooves together.

Life lived in community is joy doubled and grief halved.

The family of friends and loved ones we create for ourselves is the foundation for *everything* else we do in our lives. Their unconditional love and support help us love ourselves, push us to follow our dreams, and give us a soft place to land when we fall. They provide loving honesty, limitless encouragement, the perfect amount of sarcasm and humor, and the belief in our abilities when we can't see the good stuff ourselves. Treasure the family you are building right now. We can all accomplish so much more when we have someone holding our hand for support. We're all in this together.

Get To It

You've got your own team—people who love you and want to help you. It might not be the biggest team, but that's okay! You're far better off having two incredible allies than having five so-so friends. A big part of loving who God made you to be is finding the people who *deserve* to be on your team and then letting them love you. It can be tough to find your people though!

Family first. Perhaps you were blessed enough to be born into a ready-made team. I sure was. My immediate family has always been there for me unconditionally. But not everyone has a family like that. If your parents or siblings aren't people you can trust, you don't have to give them a spot in your inner circle.

Keep growing. Feel like your team isn't big enough or doesn't meet your needs? Seek out new friends who value the same things you do, who have the same sense of humor, the same general sense of right and wrong. If you aren't finding those people easily, switch up your routine. Find a local meetup for an activity you love (kickball, running, baking, hiking), or try a few different churches and see if one makes you feel more at home. Try out different gym classes or hang at a new coffee shop. Volunteer for an organization that aligns with your views. The more you put yourself out there, the more people you'll meet. Make a list of places to visit in your search for your team.

Get close. It does no good to have an excellent team if you keep them at arm's length, too afraid to let them see you at your most vulnerable. It's so important to have a support system that can be there for you through everything big and small, pretty and not so pretty. Let your people in. What have you been hiding from your team? Time to open up and ask for help!

Be discerning. As important as it is to find your people, it's just as important to know when someone doesn't belong in the family you're building for yourself. I'm not saying to cut someone out for making a mistake or for a misunderstanding—that sort of thing happens between even the best of friends. But anyone who regularly makes you feel bad about yourself, seems to be constantly competing with you, talks behind your back, lies to you, or shoots down your dreams does not deserve a spot on your team. You have only so much time and energy, and it's an absolute waste to give it to someone who doesn't value you. Just because someone is an old friend doesn't mean they're a quality friend.

Set boundaries. You don't owe anyone access to your heart, especially if they have already proven they can't be trusted with it. Once you've decided to set boundaries, stick with them. You may need to have some tough conversations, but you can do it! Stay calm and kind, honest and firm. If a friend has really hurt you and genuinely apologizes, do your best to forgive, if only for your own sake, because carrying around hurt and anger can mess with your head. Forgiving someone does not mean you have to let them back in to repeat hurtful behaviors.

Stay humble. If *you've* hurt someone, apologize—and make sure you mean it. You don't want to close out any relationship that was once important to you with regrets. Once you've done what is needed to make your bad behavior right and to set clear boundaries for the future, perhaps you can tentatively move forward in that relationship. Or you may need to lovingly let it go.

CHAPTER 10

My Kind of People

HELPING OTHERS HELPS YOU TOO

Who are your kind of people? Mine are authentic, honest, fun, sarcastic, welcoming, and generous. They know who they are, and they aren't afraid to put themselves out there. My kind of people are always ready to lend a helping hand and love their neighbors. There are a lot of different kinds of people in the world. And thank God for that! Some of us are conservative. Some of us are liberal. Some of us play it safe. Some of us like to take a lot of risks. Some have a PhD, some have a GED, and some of us have a little ADD. How boring would it be if we all looked and acted alike and were into the exact same things? Our differences make life fun and exciting.

> OUR
> *DiFFeReNCeS*
> MAKE LIFE FUN
> AND EXCITING.

But despite all of our differences, we all have more in common than you might realize. I think we all want to leave this world a little better than we found it, we all want to love and be loved, and at some point or another, we all need a little help. And if we all need help sometimes, doesn't it make sense that we should all be giving our help freely whenever we can? I think so.

GENTLE RONNIE

Growing up, I spent a lot of time with my cousin Ronnie. We both loved to roller-skate and swim, watch cartoons, and play on the swing set at the park. We were the best of friends. I was six and he was sixty. Ronnie was born with an intellectual disability, the sweetest, kindest, gentlest soul I've ever known, and I thought he hung the moon.

As I grew older, I witnessed firsthand how badly Ronnie was treated at times. It felt like so many people didn't see Ronnie as a real person. People made hurtful comments within earshot, pushed ahead of him to get to the front of lines, or spoke to my family about him as if he wasn't standing right there listening the whole time. It was really tough to watch people be unkind to him. I couldn't tell if he really noticed or if it bothered him, but it bothered me. I talked to my mom about it, sobbing and pouring out my heart.

"Well," she said, "we just have to be an example to other people of how he should be treated."

I still carry those words with me everywhere I go. My mom was just talking about Ronnie, but I think that's true of everyone.

When I went to elementary school, there was a little girl with Down syndrome. She was so loving and always wanted to hug and kiss us. Other kids would be grossed out, but I'd let her kiss me because she reminded me of Ronnie. I wanted to be an example to the other kids of how she should be treated. Having Ronnie in my family, and especially having such a close bond with him, really gave me a deeper understanding of people with intellectual disabilities and how much love and respect they deserve. I also understand that if you haven't spent time with someone like Ronnie, you might not know *how* to be the type of friend they need.

When I was in sixth grade, I was finally old enough to volunteer for the Special Olympics in my hometown. I worked with a group of kids for four years after that, and they were like *my* kids. If you messed with them, you were messing with me! One of those girls, Bayle, still keeps in touch after all this time. She comes to see me perform every time I appear at the Grand Ole Opry, and I'm always so excited to see her smiling face.

FINDING A BIGGER PURPOSE

Something about volunteering gave me a sense of purpose, even as a little girl. I loved helping those kids feel a sense of accomplishment through sports and getting to celebrate with them when they crossed the finish line. If this whole singing thing hadn't worked out, I was planning to pursue a career in special education. If my career disappeared tomorrow, you can bet I'd be applying to colleges to become a teacher or social worker.

So when I had a meeting with my agency after *American Idol* ended and they asked, "What kinds of companies or brands would you like to work with?" I had my answer ready to go. I was only sixteen years old at that point, so I'm sure they were probably expecting me to say Forever 21 or car companies. Instead, I said, "Well I'd really like to work with the Special Olympics." Luckily, that was a quick call and the Special Olympics invited me to become an ambassador for Project UNIFY, which brings youth with and without intellectual disabilities together through education, sports, and related initiatives to provide them with the knowledge, attitudes, and skills necessary to create and sustain school communities that promote the acceptance, respect, and human dignity for all students.

My job was to assist the Special Olympics' efforts to raise awareness and to change the attitudes of youth toward people with intellectual disabilities who struggle to be accepted, heard, and included in society. But I was also invited to attend the world games, which were in Pyeong Chang, South Korea, that year. I was thrilled. I got to meet all of those amazing athletes who worked so hard and were so excited to be there. You don't understand how much it truly means to them until you're there and you watch it firsthand. To see people from all different countries come together and support each other and to see their smiling faces as they're competing . . . it's incredible.

Nothing makes me happier or inspires me more than spending time with the athletes. I actually got to participate in a winter sport, which I will never forget. I definitely got last place (sorry to my partner!). But that didn't matter. I had a blast and it showed me just how much training and skill and strength these athletes bring to the table. If I could load up everybody in the world and take them to the games to see what goes on there, I would. It's incredible.

The Special Olympics will always have a piece of my heart, but I have also supported other charities and initiatives, including St. Jude Children's Research Hospital, Breast Cancer Awareness, State Farm's Neighborhood of Good, ACM Lifting Lives, Second Harvest Food Bank, Friends Life, Big Brothers and Big Sisters of Tennessee, Musicians on Call, and others. There are so many incredible charities doing great work out there and so many that are based right in my backyard in Nashville. I wanted to find a way to be more intentional about partnering with those charities and making it a regular part of my schedule, not just waiting for a charity to approach me with an opportunity.

So with the help of my team, I launched my own foundation, My Kinda People. I didn't think we needed to create a brand-new charity—not with so many amazing options already out there—we just needed to find a way to lift up the charities that were already out there doing such good work. So we partner with charities, both big and small, to help raise awareness and money for them and to share their stories through my platform. We got the name from a song I'd written for *The Road Less Traveled* album that was all about being kind to people and not judging them by the way they look, the color of their skin, how tall or short they are, or what background they come from. It felt like the right message for what we are trying to do with My Kinda People.

BE SOMEONE ELSE'S KIND OF PERSON

You know, we're all in this together. Our world isn't a perfect place. A lot of people out there are hurting, struggling, doing everything they can to make it through (you might be one of those people). A natural disaster, a health crisis, or even, yes, a pandemic can throw an otherwise stable family off course. When one of us falls or needs help, it's up to the rest of us to offer a hand up. I truly, truly believe that we are called to help one another whenever and however we can. If I can help lighten even one person's burden, I want to make that happen.

I TRULY, TRULY

BELIEVE THAT WE ARE

CALLED TO HELP

ONE ANOTHER

WHENEVER AND

HOWEVER WE CAN.

A million things are happening every single day and we're all going through stuff, but no matter how crazy our lives are, I think it's really important to look at what the people around us need and to lift them up however we can. I have the most amazing and unique job that allows me to travel all over the world. Every place I've visited has been full of people doing God's good work and caring for one another. I have been privileged to meet so many of those people and hear their stories. Some of those stories are uplifting and some stories are painful, but all of them have touched me and left a lasting impression.

The truth of the matter is that we all have a story.

I have found it to be very helpful to use my story and my experiences as an influence on which charities I partner with. If volunteering seems like foreign territory to you, and you don't know where to start, I would encourage you to really think about the things that have affected your life, and look for foundations, causes, and charities that relate to what you've been through. I have been able to raise awareness and money for people with intellectual disabilities, children who grew up in homes with addiction, women who have been in relationships with an addict, people with eating disorders, and a number of cancer organizations. The causes that speak to me may not be the same as the ones that speak to you. If you don't know where to begin, looking at your life and what you've been through is a good place to start.

We all have setbacks in life. We all have moments when we need help. And we all have beautiful moments when we are able to help someone else. Your stories and my stories, all those moments are woven together; we are all in it together. Find a way to be a part of someone in need's story today.

Get To It

I have some great news: you don't have to be famous or have a huge following on Instagram to make a real difference in the lives of people in your community. Every organization needs three things:

- Time
- Donations
- Exposure

If you're insanely busy, maybe you can give money or supplies. If you're cash poor, you can spread awareness about a charity you believe in via social media. And you can always, always volunteer your time. No matter what season of life you're in, there is a way you can help.

I've found that a lot of people who didn't grow up working with charities feel a little uncomfortable stepping up or think it's going to be super boring. It's true that volunteering can take us out of our comfort zones, but there are plenty of opportunities available that will be right in your sweet spot.

If you don't feel connected to the elderly, you don't have to volunteer at a nursing home. If addiction is triggering for you, it probably wouldn't be the best idea to sign up to help at a halfway house. And that is 100 percent okay. I started volunteering for the Special Olympics because it's a cause I believe in and because I felt really comfortable around kids with special needs. Start where you feel comfortable. It will be far easier to connect with the people you're there to help if you feel relaxed and engaged.

Start by identifying a few causes that speak to your heart.

- Are there articles you've read about an injustice that just made you so mad you could spit?
- Is there something you've seen on the news that made you feel like your heart was breaking?
- Are there organizations you already support, but you'd like to do more?
- Is there a disease, issue, or circumstance that has had a big impact on your life? Something you already feel equipped to help with?
- After you've given your time to a community or cause, how do you feel? Have any of your perspectives changed?

That anger, grief, conviction—a.k.a. passion—is what will make you a great volunteer for that particular cause. And I believe that God puts that passion in our hearts to lead us to His purpose for us, the things He is calling us to accomplish or help with. When you find those things that spark your passion and fuel your feelings of purpose, you'll know.

Once you've found somewhere to help, reach out to see what that organization really needs. Sometimes they just need a few specific jobs done, but at other times they're looking to take advantage of their volunteers' strengths and gifts. If you're great with kids or a chopping superstar in the kitchen, offer to tackle the jobs that allow you to use those talents. Taking something you're great at and combining it with a group you're excited to help pays off in big ways. But there is really no wrong way to volunteer. I mean it. All of the jobs are important jobs, no matter how mundane or unglamorous, because they allow the organization to help people who really need it.

There are always opportunities to help carry someone's burden right in your own neighborhood. You can reach out to lend a hand anytime you see a friend or neighbor struggling. Find ways to help that feel right to you.

- Offer to mow the lawn of your neighbor going through chemo.
- Pick up litter on your block.
- Bake brownies for your local fire department.
- Drop off a meal for the new mom down the street.
- Pay for the order of the car behind you in the drive-through line.
- Grab a few extra boxes of mac 'n' cheese at the store to donate to the local food bank.
- Clean out your closet and donate gently used items to a shelter in town.
- Pay off a few delinquent lunch accounts at your child's school.
- Walk the mail up to your elderly neighbor's door.

I also want to encourage you to give of your time whenever you can. My schedule can be absolutely bonkers, especially when I'm on tour, but I have fans who reach out to me with volunteer opportunities all the time, and I love to join them in their towns to help out when I'm on the road. Don't keep those opportunities a secret—tell me, tell your friends, tell your coworkers! My fans have turned me on to some incredible organizations, and seeing their passion for making their communities kinder, warmer places to live always inspires me.

I make volunteering a priority because—and I can't stress this enough—it really is just as rewarding for the person giving as it is for the person receiving. I just absolutely love it and I know you will too. When someone lends a helping hand to someone else in need, both people win. The person who receives help feels overwhelming love and gratitude, and the helper feels overwhelming love and pride.

Discovering your passions and your purpose will help you know and love yourself better than ever before. Even when my self-esteem has been at its lowest, getting out of my own head and connecting with people I can help has softened my heart toward myself. Seeing myself through the eyes of someone I was loving on helped show me that I was worthy of love too. I am at my very best when I am helping, connecting, and loving. I love that version of myself. I want you to find that version of yourself, too, because loving others helps you love yourself.

CHAPTER 11

GeTTiNG GooD

BE WHERE YOUR FEET ARE

hen I was fifteen years old, Juicy Couture velour sweat suits were all the rage. They were low-rise bell-bottomed sweatpants with the word *Juicy* printed boldly across the rear with a matching cropped jacket with a hood. It felt like everybody who was anybody had them, from the girls I went to school with to all the really rich and famous girls in magazines. I wanted one so badly, but I couldn't afford one. There was just no way that my mama was going to give me more than $150 for a matching sweat suit that didn't even fully cover my stomach. No chance.

I thought if I could just make enough money to buy one of those sweat suits, I'd finally look the way I wanted to feel—famous, stylish, and successful. So after I went on *American Idol*, well, I strutted my stuff right down to the mall and bought myself a hot pink velour Juicy sweat suit.

I looked ridiculous in it.

First of all, this thing was not just pink. It was stop-you-in-your-tracks, shockingly bright hot pink. See-it-in-the-dark hot pink. And second of all, I realized why those pants were called juicy—because my thighs looked *way* too juicy in that outfit.

Those sweat suits looked so cute on so many girls, but they just weren't for me. I wanted to look like I'd made it, but it turns out I was better off with the clothes I already had, which were styles I liked that worked well for my body. I'm sure you've experienced something similar. Did you dream about Juicy Couture too? Come on . . . you can be honest here. Or was there some other thing you wanted for ages, but when you finally got it, it just fell flat? Maybe it wasn't a physical object for you. Maybe it was a dream job. Or accomplishing an important goal.

BEING CONTENT

I am a very goal-oriented person and always have been. I get restless easily and want to be out there getting something done. Give me a challenge to tackle or a to-do list to check off, and I'll hit the ground running. And once I've completed one goal, I'm ready to move on to the next one. I've always felt like if I could just push a little harder and do a little more, I'd finally feel successful, happy, complete. But each accomplishment, no matter how good it feels at first, eventually loses its shine and leaves me restless again.

When I was younger, I thought if I could get my song to number one on country radio, or if I could be on tour with a big name, or if I could headline my own tour, I'd finally feel like I had made it in my career. Or maybe if I found a handsome, successful boyfriend, I'd finally be blissfully happy. Perhaps if I bought my first house or had a certain amount of money in the bank, I'd finally feel secure.

I thought I'd be happy if I could make those things reality, that they'd somehow make me feel more fulfilled in who I am.

Well, I've accomplished plenty of those. And while

I'm proud and it did feel good at the time, those achievements didn't magically fix everything. The hard truth is that if you aren't happy right now, you won't be happy when you reach that goal. Because you will still be you— just with a promotion or a bigger house or a nicer car or a pair of Juicy sweats that don't look so good on you. You'll still have the same insecurities, the same doubts, and be just as hard on yourself. If you don't feel content with who you are and what you have today, you won't be more content *tomorrow* with who you might be or what you might have. The secret to happiness isn't achieving more; it's deciding to be happy right now, shifting your mindset to embrace where you are and what you have in this moment.

IT'S ABOUT GRATITUDE

It's great to have goals. It's great to know where you want to go. That's important when it comes to getting things done in your life. But it's also important to take time to really see what you have right now. When I take time to do that, I see my wonderful home I just bought in Nashville, which took a lot of hard work. I see my two

IF YOU AREN'T
HAPPY NOW,
YOU WON'T BE HAPPY
WHEN YOU REACH
THAT GOAL.

beautiful nephews, who are precious little angels that my brother and his wife, Baylie, gifted to the world. I see my amazing support system of trusted friends and family. I see my career, my absolute dream come true of a job that allows me to make and share my music (and get paid for it)! And even though there are things about my career and my personal life that I wish were in a different place, I'm still so grateful for where they are today.

All the wonderful things in my life right now? They were goals and dreams I had for myself. Isn't that crazy to think about? Fifteen-year-old Lauren was *hoping and wishing* for the career success I take for granted some days! While eighteen-year-old Lauren was sitting in a small apartment trying to scrape enough together to pay rent, she couldn't even fathom owning a home like I do now. The Lauren of two years ago was down on her knees praying for God to heal her broken heart and give her the strength to make something beautiful from her breakup. Releasing *Getting Over Him*, a mini album of songs I wrote out of that breakup, was the answer to those prayers. And I am so proud of every single one of those songs.

For the sake of each of those Laurens from the past, I really need to appreciate these achievements and soak them up. I worked hard for these things. I should take time to celebrate and be grateful before moving to the next thing on my list. Your other dreams still matter, but try to acknowledge and enjoy what you have right now.

It's not a simple thing to shift a mindset you may have held for a long time, but there are some things you can do to help you embrace gratitude and focus on the now.

1. *Count your blessings.* There's a reason that was your grandmother's favorite piece of advice—it works! Acknowledging all the wonderful things you have *right this minute* will help you see more clearly that your life is already full of goodness. Whether it's your loving family or friendships, your job, your pets, your faith, the roof over your head, or the car in your driveway, we can *all* find something to be thankful for, even if it's just one thing.

2. *Be mindful.* I like to start each day by thanking God for everything He's given me. Our thoughts have power. Focusing on and praying about the good stuff means you'll notice more good stuff. And when you notice more good stuff, you'll start to find *even more* good stuff. That gratitude will

flow into every part of your life, and you'll want to focus on the present because you'll want to enjoy all the gifts you see right now.

3. *Write it down*. Still struggling? Get a pretty journal and write down everything you're thankful for every day. Sometimes writing it down can help it stick in our brains better. And when you find yourself playing the "If only I had" game, you can go back to your journal and read all of the things you already have, which should help bring perspective. I do that as part of my songwriting process, and it helps keep me on track.

4. *Take a break*. My next suggestion may be unpopular, but hear me out. Take a big break from social media, magazines, blogs, and podcasts for a bit, at least from the ones that push you into the comparison pit. You know which ones I mean. The women on Instagram with the perfectly decorated and clean homes, the perfect husbands, and the perfectly adorable kids and dogs. The talented girls dancing on TikTok with all the moves and perfect hair. The podcast that offers more tips than you can handle to make your life perfectly efficient and optimized.

INTERNET VS. REALITY

We have access to unlimited curated, filtered, and sponsored content online. And it seems fun at first. But over time it can make you feel "less than" when you look at your own imperfect, messy life. We may know in our heads that the stuff online isn't the whole picture—that there's a pile of junk off-camera, that it took all day to get that dance right—but our hearts, our sweet, sensitive hearts, are more easily fooled.

Trust me, I don't always look like I do in my Instagram pictures. I have a glam squad to get me ready for those social media photos. Of course I look perfectly polished! If you see me at the grocery store, you'll likely see me in an oversized T-shirt, a messy bun, and no makeup. Not the same at all.

And I struggle too. I noticed that I was doing most of my social media scrolling late at night, before bed, and it was draining away all the joy and excitement I'd experienced that day (and setting a bad tone before drifting off to sleep). So I set a boundary for myself. I put a lock on all the apps on my phone from 9:00 p.m. to 8:00 a.m. so I wouldn't be tempted to open them. Of course, I can override that lock if I absolutely must check something, but having to go through the override process makes me think about whether I *really* need to do it before I open the app. Nine times out of ten, I decide not to open the app. Instead, I'll pick up a book or do some other activity. It's a small thing, but it has made a big difference in how contented and grateful I feel with what I have and where I'm at.

When we fall into comparing our *very real lives* to those *very unreal* filtered, staged, edited images and videos, it yanks our minds and hearts out of all the good stuff we've got going on. It makes us feel like we aren't good enough—that is not who God says we are, and it's not helping us love ourselves either. It drops us right back into thinking, *If I had her house, I'd be happy*, or, *If I had her job and her wardrobe, I'd feel fulfilled*. I promise you that the grass is not actually greener over there—it's just that Perpetua filter she used on the photo!

THE GRASS IS GREENEST WHERE WE WATER IT.

The grass is greenest where we water it. When we are able to focus on all the precious gifts already in our lives, we are happier, more content, and more able to accept and love ourselves. You may find this hard to believe, but I can almost guarantee someone out there is looking at *you* and wishing they had what you have.

MINDSET MATTERS

It takes work, but it is so worth it to change your mindset to focus on what you already have instead of on what you don't. Cultivating a more grateful heart and avoiding comparison will really help you see all the ways you can grow right where you're planted. My life is already so rich and wonderful, and I don't want to miss out on a minute of it because I'm distracted by what I don't have or what might happen in the future. I hope you feel the same way.

My dad's about to celebrate another year of being sober from alcoholism, which is such a blessing. I want to celebrate that and be proud and thankful instead of worrying that he'll take a drink tomorrow. My nephews are six and three years old. I want to soak in every moment of their cuteness and enjoy them as they are right now. Before I know it, Bradey won't be calling spaghetti "pisgetti" anymore or calling me "Wawa" instead of "Lala," and Bentley won't be begging me to snuggle before he falls asleep. I don't want to miss out on that preciousness because I'm already worrying about how they'll handle bullies in middle school. On a girl's trip, I want to soak up the late-night conversations over margaritas and queso instead of thinking about how rare these trips will become once we're all married and having babies. So let's live each day instead of rushing through them. My journey has been such a beautiful one, even at its hardest, and it's important to appreciate that beauty as we go.

Each of our journeys will look different, and that is a beautiful thing. Definitely set your goals and go after them, but don't forget to enjoy the journey along the way. Ditch the comparisons, soak up the joy of each season, and thank God that your life's already good.

Get To It

If you look around at your life, I'm sure you'll see things you used to wish and pray for and the results of goals you've already accomplished.

- Isn't it amazing to see the proof that you can do hard things? What are some big goals you've already made happen for yourself?
- Do you have any mementos or pictures

from those accomplishments? Do you have a spot where you can display them to help you stay motivated?

I know it gives me a big ol' confidence boost when I see the dress I wore to accept the ACM Award for New Female Artist of the Year or when I walk into my music room and see all the plaques for my number-one hits. Those might just be things, but they bring me so much joy because they remind me of just how far I've come.

If you have meaningful reminders like that, put them out where you can see them.

- Dust off that diploma and hang it on your wall!
- Put that trophy on your bookshelf.
- Hang up those marathon medals and ribbons.
- Frame that picture of you on your first day at your dream job.
- Display the quilt you sewed in your living room for guests to admire.

You earned those things through hard work, grit, and perseverance. You likely failed a lot along the way and learned in the process. Recognizing where we've been and what we've already done is a great way to remind us to enjoy all of the cool things we're doing today that will be happy memories one day.

Whether it's comparison or knocking out goals or just plain busyness, a lot can take us out of the moment and make us feel anxious about what's to come. It might help to adopt a phrase to remind you to live in the moment. Mine is "one bite at a time." I was panicking once about how to handle everything, and my manager asked, "How do you eat an elephant, Lauren?" I, of course, said, "I don't know." And she replied, "One bite at a time." It cracked me up, and I've been saying it ever since to remind me to take things as they come.

Pick a phrase for yourself. You're welcome to steal mine, but you could also go with:

- Soak it up.
- Be here now.

- One day at a time.
- Life's already good.
- Being present matters.
- I am here.
- I am present.
- Little by little is how big things get done.
- This is the moment that matters.
- This is it.
- Here and now is everything.
- I'm making space for now.

It doesn't matter what you say; it only matters that saying it helps you focus on the here and now so that you can truly enjoy it.

CHAPTER 12

**CHASE AFTER THE PERSON
YOU WANT TO BE**

*L*ife moves so fast. It can be easy to get caught up in all the busyness and forget to be intentional about doing the things that truly matter to us. We all have dreams and goals burning inside us, things we feel called to accomplish. It's up to each of us to make those things happen for ourselves. We have to be both dreamers and doers.

We all have different journeys, sure, different paths, dreams, goals, hopes, and fears. But we were all born to

187

be who God designed us to be. And I think one of the biggest challenges any of us will ever face is to take the chance on being who God made us to be.

You already know, deep down, what that means for you. Who God made you to be is the version of you who doesn't try to live up to anyone else's expectations. The version of you who knows herself and isn't willing to compromise who she is for anyone else. She's the version of you who loves herself boldly and fully and likes herself too. She's the version of you who stands up for herself, knows exactly what she wants, and sings her own praises. She doesn't need anyone to tell her she's awesome, amazing, or worthy—she already knows she is. It took me nearly twenty-five years to find that version of me, and I'm never letting her go again.

I've never regretted, not for even a single second, going after my dreams with everything I've got. It has been difficult at times—so, so difficult—but it has always been worth it. It meant believing in myself even when no one else seemed to, when my record label didn't like my songs, when I had to sell my car and skip meals because I was flat broke, when the singles I put out languished midway up the charts and barely got radio play, when I took every appearance offered just to pay my rent.

If I hadn't believed in myself, it would have been far easier to give up on those dreams because it was *just too hard*. I easily could have chosen a job as a waitress or gone to college to become a teacher or moved back home to get married and start having babies. There were wider, easier, different paths I could have chosen, and no one would have blamed me for giving up on my big dream. But I would have blamed myself.

> WE HAVE TO BE BOTH *DREAMERS* AND *DOERS*.

Only you know which of your dreams are the big ones, the ones worth chasing to the end, the ones your heart will never let go of. But in order to really know that clearly, you have to know yourself and what God made you for.

And you have to love yourself enough not to give up on you.

Some of us find our dreams when we're young (I'd been imagining myself on *American Idol* since I was six), but not everyone does. There's no right or wrong season of life to find a dream. If you aren't really sure what your big dream is yet, that's okay. Keep learning about yourself and doing the things you love, the things that bring you joy, and you'll find those big dreams on your heart. Some people don't find their big dreams until midlife or after retiring. It's truly never too late!

I think sometimes people believe that their dreams have to be big and flashy, but they don't. Maybe your dream is becoming a mom or starting your own small business in your hometown or mastering a certain skill. Maybe you fantasize about landing a job at a specific company you really admire. Maybe you dream of helping special-needs kids or working at a nonprofit you really believe in. These dreams are the ones that make a big difference in the world. And they matter every bit as much as the fame-and-fortune dreams (often even more!). If everyone dreamed of being famous, *whoo boy*, would our world be in trouble! We need all different kinds of people dreaming all different types of dreams to make our world the best it can be.

If you already have a dream, don't hold back. Life is happening right now, and if you wait, you may miss out. I know going for it can be scary. What if you fail? What if everyone laughs at you? What if your dream doesn't work out? Going from dreamer to doer is not for the faint of heart. But isn't it worth it to try instead of living the rest of your life afraid of all of those "what ifs"? I was scared too—terrified actually—but I believed in myself and I needed to know if I could make my dreams real. If I failed, I failed, but I had to know. Don't you want to know?

There's one "what if" that people always forget when they let fear stop them from going after their dreams: *What if you succeed?* Our dreams can be achieved with hard work and perseverance and faith in ourselves. What will you do if your biggest dreams come true? Will you remember to be grateful? Will you steward those gifts well?

I believe that our biggest, dearest dreams come from God. I believe He gives us our dreams to help us discover just what we're capable of and to help us grow into the people He created us to be. The process of chasing our dreams challenges us, tests us, and refines us into stronger, more confident, and more faithful versions of ourselves. Yes, we achieve something we can be proud of. But the real growth comes from the process, not the achievement.

That's what pushes us to our limits and then shows us that we can sail past them.

That's what challenges our beliefs about our own abilities and reveals new strengths and talents.

That's what helps us see who our real friends are and aren't.

GOING FROM

DREAMER TO DOER

IS NOT FOR THE

FAINT OF HEART.

That's what shows us what we are capable of on our own and just how much we all need God to come alongside us.

THIS HOLY HOT MESS

All the stories I've shared in this book are a collection of lessons and discoveries that have made me who I am today. Some were sad. Some were painful. Some were exhilarating. Some were joyous. Some are still teaching me. And they're all part of my journey—a journey I'm so proud and grateful to have traveled.

Looking back on my life, although I think we all wish certain hardships hadn't happened, I can honestly say that I wouldn't change a thing. Even the experiences that were crushing ultimately caused me to grow. And God was always there to put me back together, stronger than before. Without hardship, I wouldn't know just how deep my faith is—in myself and in God. Yes, I've looked foolish at times. But I've come out the other side a survivor, equipped to love and respect myself and my body, to love others well, to fight for what's right, to be confident in my resilience. I've also experienced times of life-changing joy, true peace that can come only from God, and a deep sense of creative purpose that I wouldn't trade for anything.

My country music dreams have always been part of that purpose. God gave me a voice and a love of music, and I know He wants me to use it to reach all different kinds of people. I've been able to share my heart and my struggles to help others. And as much as I love music, I think the most important part of what I do is connecting with my fans. Using the voice I've been given to inspire, encourage, and share the truth of Jesus with people all over the world is my purpose, and I wouldn't be able to live that out if I hadn't achieved my dream of becoming a singer and songwriter.

It all boils down to us and this holy hot mess of a life we've been given. We have to choose to love ourselves, to believe in who God made us to be, to trust ourselves, and to make the leap and get after this big life waiting for us. We have to choose to see the beauty in the journey and learn as much as possible on the way. We have to choose to embrace our paths and to be proud of where they're taking us. And we have to choose to fight for ourselves.

We all get only one chance at this whole life thing. One chance on this earth to make our mark. One chance to do good. One chance to be fully ourselves.

Let's not waste it! Run after you. Chase after who you are meant to be. Run toward knowing yourself, the real you. Run toward finding your people, your team. Run toward accomplishing your goals and your dreams. Run toward knowing God.

And most of all, run toward loving yourself.

Because when you can stand up and shout out, "I love myself!" and mean it, nothing will be able to stop you from living your best life.

And I'm here rooting you on every step of the way.

With love,

Lauren

ABOUT THE AUTHOR

Lauren Alaina is a platinum-selling country music star who broke out in the tenth season of *American Idol*. Her awards include 2017 ACM New Female Vocalist of the Year, CMT Breakthrough Video of the Year for "Road Less Traveled," and CMT Collaborative Video of the Year for "What Ifs," the 6x platinum-selling #1 hit with childhood friend Kane Brown. Lauren has received multiple nominations for ACM Awards, CMA Awards, CMT Music Awards, Teen Choice Awards, Radio Disney Awards, and Billboard Music Awards. She's also the host of *Jesus Calling: Stories of Faith* on Circle TV.